Howling Up to the Sky

The Opioid Epidemic

Edited by Jaynie Royal and Ruth Feiertag

Anthology Copyright © 2018 Regal House Publishing

Edited by Jaynie Royal and Ruth Feiertag

First published in 2018 by Pact Press, an imprint of
Regal House Publishing, LLC
Raleigh, NC 27612
All rights reserved

Printed in the United States of America

ISBN -13 (paperback): 978-1-9475483-2-9
ISBN -13 (epub): 978-1-9475483-3-6
Library of Congress Control Number: 2018930047

Interior design by Lafayette & Greene
Cover design by Lafayette & Greene
lafayetteandgreene.com
Cover art by Mikadun/Shutterstock

Pact Press
www.pactpress.com
Regal House Publishing, LLC
https://regalhousepublishing.com

All net proceeds from the sale of this anthology, without a maximum cap, are donated to the Shatterproof for the duration of time that this work is in print. This nonprofit organization was selected due to its dedication to relieving the suffering associated with addiction. As its mission stipulates:

Shatterproof is a national nonprofit organization dedicated to ending the devastation addiction causes families.

Shatterproof
www.shatterproof.org

Additional donations can be sent directly to the Shatterproof at:

Shatterproof
135 West 41st Street, 6th Floor
New York, NY 10036

Contents

Acknowledgements

Any book is a work of collaboration and co-operation, but an anthology, especially one expedited to speak in a timely manner to an ongoing nightmare, requires exceptional efforts from many people to see the light of day. We cannot thank the contributors to this volume adequately. Many of them bared their souls in their desire to prevent addiction and heal the wounds caused by this scourge. There is real risk in announcing to the world that one suffers from this affliction and we stand in awe of our authors' courage and compassion. All were responsive to our truncated time-table and turned around their revisions at warp speed.

We owe huge and particular thanks to Alma McKinley and Anna Schoenbach for joining us in writing an effective introduction that provides the background readers need to bring to the articles, stories, and poems contained in this volume. Without their invaluable research, *Howling Up to the Sky* would be a much less cogent contribution to the discussion raging through our society about this epidemic and how to find effective and humane solutions for it.

We also want to acknowledge the inspiration provided by Shatterproof and Roots of Recovery, two groups facing down the storm and offering different kinds of refuge to addicts and others affected by the ravages of the opioids that are coursing through the body of our country. Their heroic efforts cannot be overstated.

Gobs of gratitude go to Avery Feiertag for his perspicacious observations and assistance in the late stages of preparing this manuscript. Especially since he was supposed to be on vacation.

And finally, exceptional and abundant gratitude goes to Jeffrey Royal who, if he is not careful, is likely to become the *sine qua non* of Regal House Publishing.

Ruth Feiertag
Boulder, Colorado

Jaynie Royal
Raleigh, North Carolina

Forward

— Catherine McDowell —

I have been in the center of the addiction crisis and battleground of recovery since 1984. In 2016, while working with a group of women, the concept of Roots of Recovery began to develop. Our mission is to offer a peer support program for women who have become hopeless, helpless, and homeless. At Roots of Recovery, we are building a cottage community to serve women with alcohol and other drug addictions and their children.

Opioid overdose deaths more than quadrupled between 1999 and 2014, and have only continued to rise in recent years. In total, more than 63,000 Americans died of drug overdoses in 2016, according to the latest data from the U.S. Centers for Disease Control and Prevention (CDC NCHS Data Brief No. 294, December 2017). Numbers like this have created what is now known as the "Opioid Crisis."

This crisis has been a long time coming, and it is not the first of its kind. Over the past fifty years, a period that sometimes seems like only a blink of the eye, a number of different substances have held the position of society's most-favored drug of choice. We have passed through the 1960s, which were influenced by the popularization of LSD and, in the 1970s, marijuana grew in popularity. Powder cocaine became the trend in the 1980s, which morphed into the crack epidemic of the 1990s. We welcomed the millennium with methamphetamine destroying families across the country. By 2010 we were a nation addicted to pain relievers and left us today standing at the center of the "Opioid Epidemic."

We have to ask ourselves what have we learned and why has nothing changed in the last fifty years. Those answers do not lie entirely with the medical profession, but with changes in how we treat and think about addiction. If we look at the road which leads to opioid addiction for many people, beginning with first being prescribed opioids for chronic pain relief, in many cases, opioid prescriptions aren't well suited to the conditions for which they were prescribed. In long-term studies of opioid use for lower back pain, for example, opioids don't work very well at relieving pain. (JAMA Intern Med. 2016;176(7):958-968. doi:10.1001/jamainternmed.2016.1251).

We have to look at our society as a whole and the changes in our livelihoods, family structure, and societal pressures. Those afflicted with Substance Use Disorder, use essentially to obtain the ease and comfort that comes at once with the next use. As opioids became much more prevalent in society, many who took them also noticed and enjoyed the obvious side effects. Opioids have a profound impact on the brain, including facilitating sleep and reducing anxiety, leaving many people to feel a sense of well-being after taking them. It's that relief from suffering that appealed to most people, who perhaps didn't realize they were plagued by more than a physical injury.

The question for our society today is "How do we navigate

our way out this latest crisis?" The first giant hurdle we must overcome is the stigma associated with Substance Use Disorder. The concept of stigma describes the powerful, negative perceptions commonly associated with substance abuse and addiction. Stigma has the potential to negatively affect a person's self-esteem, damage relationships with loved ones, and prevent those suffering from addiction from accessing treatment.

Becoming dependent on drugs can happen to anyone. It's important to keep in mind that we can all do a better job of decreasing stigma around drug use. When people experience stigma regarding their drug use, they are less likely to seek treatment, and this results in economic, social, and collateral medical costs. Integrating addiction treatment into general health care settings, where addiction could be treated like other chronic conditions, would be ideal, but it's not likely to happen. Treatment is also counter to the way the medical system traditionally framed recovery from addiction. Traditionally treatment programs were designed with addiction as an acute illness, providing the typical thirty-day program. You get people in, you fix them up, and you send them out. Today, the consensus of health care professionals is that's not a realistic depiction of addiction, which is a chronic, often lifelong, condition.

In regard to addiction treatment, there is no one-size-fits-all approach. Most people don't know what treatment approach will work for them and they have to try more than one, and more than one time. Very few people find an approach that puts them into long-term recovery on the first attempt.

Given that the majority of people with addiction will need to attempt recovery multiple times, accessibility and affordability are key.

Additionally, we need to view the person as a whole within the context of his or her living environment and what is required to sustain long-term recovery.

When the country's poverty and unemployment rates are high, when childcare and safe housing are expensive, and when access to education, quality jobs, and opportunities is limited, there's a feeling despair that settles in. All of this has helped create a culture of hopelessness, which makes long-term recovery incredibly difficult. When the fear of financial insecurity and the possibility of becoming homeless becomes overwhelming, individuals will seek to find comfort the only way they feel they can, by using drugs and alcohol once more.

We need to create a more dependable system of environmental support—one that can assess the quality of recovery, not just abstinence from alcohol or drugs. So, how does global recovery look?

At Roots of Recovery, we have developed a holistic recovery program, which incorporates a mix of Peer Support Recovery practices, job and life skills training, along with access to high school and college educations. There are familiar aspects of recovery: daily twelve-step group sessions and peer support mentorships. But there are also yoga, farming, beekeeping, and cottage construction. We believe that hands-on work can be healing, and provides a sense of purpose that addiction may have taken away.

We are also invested in the creation of more robust jobs and housing infrastructure, which can give recovering women access to a variety of tools to help them resist fears that may lead back to drug use. If we don't offer women supportive housing and employment, a safe environment in which to raise their children, then that despair sets in and they don't see any other life. And if they don't see any other life, they can't face that as a life option, and they may turn to what makes them happy and comfortable, and that is the use of drugs and alcohol.

The issues of addiction and the crisis of a lack of accessible recovery supports are complicated, vast, and at times, overwhelming. This anthology asks you to stand a while on the firing line—witness the tragedies, the lives lost, the tortured families, the despairing friends, and also to experience the joy of recovery.

I ask that you remain open-minded while reading these works and examine your personal beliefs regarding addiction, its causes, and various solutions. As long as an addict has breath in her or his body and a connection to someone who cares, there is always hope for recovery.

https://www.huffingtonpost.com/entry/america-on-opioids-dispatches_us_59dbe9d9e4b0208970cf222a?ncid=inblnkushpmg00000009

https://drugabuse.com/library/addiction-stigma/

Catherine McDowell
Executive Director and founder
Roots of Recovery
June10inc

Introduction

When we first conceived of this anthology series, I think Jaynie and I didn't realize the number of issues we would want to confront, the multitude of voices needing platforms. Our first collection, *Speak and Speak Again*, highlighted a sample of the troubles that beset our nation and the psyches of some of its citizens, and it set the stage for the anthologies to follow. I hope that some time we will again collect another such diverse group, but this compendium, *Howling Up to the Sky*, is focused not on a set of disparate problems, but on a single, terrible plague: the overwhelming, seemingly inexorable opioid crisis that is permeating every facet of our society.

Within that focus, however, we present a diverse group of voices and perspectives, a display of images that coalesce into a portrait of the sufferings and heartaches involved in opioid addiction, the circumstances that can trap people in it and impediments to solutions for it, and the hopes for prevention and promises of paths out of this morass. Our title comes from the wrenching opening story, Barbara Lodge's "A Bad Night." The story brings home the agonies inflicted on the people who care about an addict, but even as it makes us sorrow along with Ms. Lodge and her family, it infuses us with compassion for the young man who is the source of the anguish and pain.

Other aspects of this portrait include experiences couched in poetry as the fittest means to express the emotions that have rocked the speakers: the loss of "Soul-Rot" by Nathanael

Stolte; the loneliness of Justin Karcher's "Screaming Really Loudly into van Gogh's Severed Ear"; the desolation of "All the Junkies on Carr Avenue" by Damien Rucci. Other pieces bring us a doctor's struggle to find ways to alleviate pain without leading a patient into a deeper hell ("A Doctor's Perspective" by Ken Benson), a pharmacist's depiction of the dilemma of her weariness in the face of never-ending prescriptions and demands for more pain-killers (Alma McKinley's "A Pharmacist's Choices and Their Impact on the Opioid Epidemic"), a description of an innovative program for women who are struggling to get clean ("Roots of Recovery" by Laura Golden), and confessional pieces like D. Ketchum's "Some Good Has Come of This."

The variety of stories only scratches the surface of the issue. The scope of the crisis is mind-boggling, its complexity a Gordian knot too tightly wound for us to slice with any one blade. As Sydney Jennings points out, "The opioid epidemic is not only the issue of addiction to opioid medication, it's also the issue of misuse, abuse and subsequent deadly overdose crisis in America. Every single day, more than ninety Americans die after overdosing on opioids and it is only getting worse."[1] Today's crisis began well over a hundred years ago, and it is worth looking back to see how the opiate pendulum was first set into motion as our nation tried to crackdown on addiction.

Throughout the nineteenth century and well into the first

---

[1] Sydney Jennings, "Is Indivior's New Drug a Game Changer for the Opioid Addiction Epidemic?" *Study Breaks,* December, 24, 2017. http://studybreaks.com/2017/12/24/indiviors-new-drug-opioid-addiction/.

part of the twentieth, wars spread morphine like wildfire as it was used to treat the pain of injured soldiers, and each war left thousands of addicted soldiers in its wake. In addition, late in the nineteenth century, heroin was extracted from morphine and was believed to be a non-addictive derivative of it. As such, it quickly became a catch-all remedy, readily accessible and frequently prescribed to treat common ailments such as coughs, diarrhea, and menstrual cramps. As a result, a new addiction was born under the guise of a beneficial medication thought to be safe because a doctor prescribed it.[2]

The Harrison Narcotics Tax Act of 1914, legislation that taxed and controlled the usage of opiates and coca leaves in the United States, was the country's first declaration of a war on drugs. It attempted to rein in addiction and drug-related crimes; instead it spawned America's first black market for drugs. During the 1920s, an estimated thirty-five thousand physicians were indicted for prescribing narcotics to their patients. So "many doctors were arrested, put on trial, and had their careers and lives destroyed"[3] that prescribers, in fear for their lives and jobs, stopped writing scripts for opiates, and people in true need of pain medication were left to suffer. Heroin became a street drug, morphine was limited to post-operative use in hospitals, and still little was understood about the *hows* and *whys* of addiction. It seemed the country's first run-in with opiates would be coming to a

---

[2] Sam Quinones, *Dreamland: The True Tale of America's Opiate Epidemic*, (New York: Bloomsbury Press, 2015), p.53.

[3] Ronald Libby, "The DEA's War on Doctors: A Surrogate for The War on Drugs," *Congressional Briefing on The Politics of Pain: Drug Policy & Patient Access to Effective Pain Treatments*, http://www.aapsonline.org/painman/paindocs2/libbystatement.pdf.

close, but they would not go quietly into that good night.

The Act delivered its crushing blow by stating that doctors could prescribe opiates only "in the course of his professional practice." This phrase was interpreted to mean that it was unlawful to prescribe opiates to addicts. Because what separates addiction from the adverse effects any patient may experience while taking an opiate, either chronically or acutely, is a very fine line, it was difficult for doctors to know whom they might legally treat.

The pendulum began to swing back again in the late 1980s. The trend of abusing prescription opioid drugs as the gateway to injecting heroin only began in the 1990s. It was back then that Purdue Pharma, the manufacturer of Oxy-Contin, touted its new extended-release form of oxycodone as non-addictive in their widely distributed marketing materials. At the same time, the medical community was receiving a new message about the under-treatment of pain in the United States. Fueled by the desire to get patients the appropriate pain relief and eliminate any undue suffering, a small contingent of physicians and researchers began speaking out about the benefits of prescribing opiates. While opioids were reserved for the treatment of pain in cancer patients or the terminally ill, millions of people were left to cope with untreated, non-cancerous pain. Advocates for the more widespread use of opioids traveled the country urging doctors to set aside their "baseless fears" that these drugs were highly addictive, calling those fears an old school of thought which had left countless patients to suffer. Purdue leveraged the message that these patients deserved relief by pushing Oxy-

Contin as the solution to this new-found "pain crisis."

Purdue was also motivated by the fact that its MS Contin was coming off patent, which meant any manufacturer could apply through the FDA for its generic equivalent to be interchangeable with the brand name product, a distinction known in the industry as an *AB-rated generic*. In OxyContin Launch Team meeting notes dated March 31, 1995, and published in the *LA Times* in May 2016, Michael Friedman, Purdue's Chief Executive at the time, said, "Inevitably, the AB-rated generic [to MS Contin] will arrive and this is why it is of extreme timely importance that we must establish OxyContin. OxyContin can cure the vulnerability of the AB-rated generic threat and that is why it is so crucial that we devote the fullest efforts now to a successful launch of OxyContin." Those same documents indicated that Purdue was not going to limit their new product just to cancer pain. Purdue had every intention of branching out into non-malignant chronic pain, a market whose origins could be traced back to the aftermath of the Harrison Narcotics Tax Act more than seventy years earlier.

Purdue's marketing was a success. Their deliberate and methodical process included minimizing the risk of opiate addiction, pushing for more aggressive treatment of non-malignant pain, and focusing efforts on a more liberal use of sustained-release opioids to primary-care physicians, a group of doctors who many experts believed were not properly trained in the treatment of pain or addiction. Barred by federal regulations from marketing their drug, a controlled substance, directly to consumers, Purdue "educated" both physicians and patients about pain through a series of videos, journals articles, and a website entitled *Partners Against Pain*. They talked up three main points on pain: that it was more widespread than previously thought, that it was treatable, and that, in most cases, the drug of choice should be an opioid. Purdue distributed and redeemed thirty-four thousand coupons for a free limited-time trial of seven to thirty days of OxyContin, and more than five thousand healthcare professionals were recruited and trained for Purdue's national speaker bureau at over forty all-expenses-paid conferences held at resorts in Florida, Arizona, and California. The company strategically plotted to target the highest opiate prescribers in the country with its marketing efforts and by 2001 had paid $40 million in bonuses to its sales reps. In OxyContin's first six years, sales grew from $44 million in 1996 to $1.5 *billion* in 2002, with the number of prescriptions filled jumping from three hundred thousand to over seven million in the same time period.[4] By 2002, six years after its launch, OxyContin accounted for 68 percent of oxycodone sales in the U.S. and by 2004, it had become the most prevalent prescription opioid abused in the United States. Purdue had broken the pendulum.

Though OxyContin *does* help people debilitated by severe pain, countless others develop an addiction to the drug. Oxycodone, the active ingredient in OxyContin, has a potential to hook people that knows no bounds—people down on

---

[4] Government Accountability Office, "Prescription Drugs: OxyContin Abuse and Diversion and Efforts to Address the Problem," GAO-04-110, December 2003, https://www.gao.gov/new.items/d04110.pdf (pg. 31).

their luck, people taking a pain pill recommended by friends or neighbors, or people looking to escape boredom or sadness for just one evening. OxyContin, meant to treat pain, has wound up being an affliction of its own, one that continues to spread across America, ravaging communities, homes, and families. Once crushed, the powder contained in a single tablet provided a high that is comparable to, if not better than, the one obtained from injecting heroin. By either dissolving or crushing the tablet, one had immediate access to pharmaceutical grade oxycodone that came with guaranteed potency, unlike its illicit street counterpart. Its popularity grew overnight. As word of mouth spread, the black market for street OxyContin exploded. The pills quickly spilled over into the streets, and from there into the hands of teenagers, amateur and professional athletes, and white- and blue-collar workers. The victims of this scourge are everywhere, and they are everyone. What doesn't occur to most of them is that the drug contained in OxyContin is practically identical to heroin in its euphoric effects and potential for addiction. People who trust what they are prescribed by their physicians become addicted. Addicts are kids who think a pill with their beer on Saturday night will just kill an otherwise lame weekend. They are once-upstanding individuals with morals and boundaries, who believed they could never have a drug or heroin problem. Eventually, taking the drug stops being about getting high or numbing pain and becomes about getting out of the low, the withdrawal. Those not on Medicaid realize within months they can't afford this habit, that their insurance won't pay for early fills, that their doctors won't write for higher doses. Faced with debilitating withdrawal symptoms, they look to the black market to relieve their suffering. Once they get priced out of buying Oxys on the street and with their bodies already ravaged by the drug, addiction wreaking havoc on their brains, these men, women, and children follow the path of least resistance, the one that brings immediate relief: injecting the less-expensive and readily available alternative, heroin.

So where are we to find hope? In stories such as Arlene's, told to us by Anna Schoenbach in her article "Beyond Pills for Pills." Ms. Schoenbach discusses the efficacy of and the debate surrounding the practice of using safer medications to help ease the pain and loosen the grip of addiction—to treat addiction, in a sense, as a chronic disease much like diabetes. But when—and whether—to end or transition away from this medication-assisted treatment is controversial. Not everyone feels that lifelong use is appropriate. "The whole concept of medication-assisted treatment," says Dr. Enid Osborne, "is that you're using one drug to replace another drug." Dr. Osborne is a public health advisor and educator in the substance abuse and addiction field. "As a person in long term recovery," Dr. Osborne continued, "I kind of have conflicting views on [medication assisted treatment]. I feel that if someone is on medication-assisted treatment, all well and good," she said. "We're saving lives, they are going into treatment—hopefully—but what about recovery? What about after?"

Dr. Osborne believes that, while medication has its place, "There has to come a time when…they're weaned off of it." Addiction, she emphasizes, is not just a chemical dependency—it is a disease of behavior, and just looking at and treating the chemical dependency, the opioid withdrawal symptoms, ignores the root causes of the person's addiction.

The urgency of these goals becomes even more imperative when we realize that "The current opioid epidemic is the deadliest drug crisis in American history. Overdoses, fueled by opioids, are the leading cause of death for Americans under 50 years old—killing roughly 64,000 people last year [2016], more than guns or car accidents, and doing so at a pace faster than the H.I.V. epidemic did at its peak."[5] Communities and the individuals that make them up can't simply wait for a solution from the top to remedy this scourge. The epidemic is challenging us to begin the hard work of stepping out of our comfort zones, engaging people at whatever place they find themselves when they're ready to seek help, and opening our eyes, minds, and hearts through education, awareness, and service. Through deliberate action everyone can make a difference.

There are individuals and organizations working to close the floodgates. Their courage and efforts have our profound admiration and, through this anthology, our support. All profits from this anthology will benefit Shatterproof, a New York-based organization that advocates for addicts and provides prevention and treatment. We must also acknowledge Roots of Recovery, a group closer to our Raleigh home, and

---

[5] Maya Salam, "The Opioid Epidemic: A Crisis Years in the Making," *New York Times* (October 26, 2017): https://www.nytimes.com/2017/10/26/us/opioid-crisis-public-health-emergency.html.

thank Catherine McDowell for her insights and for writing the forward to this anthology. Pulling together will move us over these rocky shoals more quickly than navigating alone.

In the last thirty years, pain, once only a symptom, has become a disease of its own, with conditions such as fibromyalgia, migraines, and chronic back pain costing America $635 billion annually. And since one in ten adults in this country either suffers or has suffered from on-going pain, and with the medical community continuing to rely on opioids to relieve that pain, the cost—both in money and in people—of addiction will also continue to soar. Without addressing the roots of this pain and suffering, this epidemic will continue.

And more people will die.

Jaynie Royal
Raleigh, North Carolina

Ruth Feiertag
Lafayette, Colorado

Alma McKinley
Centennial, Colorado

Anna Schoenbach
Washington, D.C.

For more information about Shatterproof, please visit https://www.shatterproof.org.

To learn more about Roots of Recovery, read Catherine McDowell's preface and Laura Golden's essay in this book, and check out the Roots of Recovery website at https://www.rootsofrecovery.org.

❧

Anna Schoenbach's Sources

1. Arlene, phone interview, (March, 2016).
2. "Behavioral Health Treatments and Services," Samhsa.gov/treatment.
3. "BHChat Corner: News You Can Use" (March 2016) Altarum Institute, http://altarum.org/about/news-and-events/bhchat-corner-news-you-can-use-march-2016.
4. "CDC Guidelines for Prescribing Opioids for Chronic Pain" Dowell et al. *Journal of the American Medical Association* (United States: March 15, 2016).
5. "Comprehensive Addiction and Recovery Act of 2016 (S. 524), as approved by the Senate Judiciary Committee on February 11, 2016: A Section-by-Section Analysis," National Association of State Alcohol and Drug Abuse Directors (February 2016), http://nasadad.org/wp-content/uploads/2016/02/CARA-Section-by-Section-Feb.-2016.pdf.
6. "Confronting an Epidemic: the Case for Eliminating Barriers to Medication-Assisted Treatment of Heroin and Opioid Addiction," Legal Action Center (March 2015),www.lac.org.
7. Enid Osborne, Project Director, SAMHA, personal communication (November 8, 2017).

8. Enid Osborne, Project Director, SAMHA, personal communication (March 15, 2016).

9. GA Enos, "Report: Better outcomes for opioid addiction lie in greater access to medication," Addictionpro.com.

10. Guo J., "The disease killing white Americans goes way deeper than opioids,"

11. *Washington Post* (March 24, 2017): https://www.washingtonpost.com/news/wonk/wp/2017/03/24/the-disease-killing-white-americans-goes-way-deeper-than-opioids/?utm_term=.4d80bb2d993e.

12. Tom Coderre, Senior advisor, Altarum Behavioral Health Technical Assistance Center, personal communication, (November 7, 2017).

13. Kolodny A, Courtwright DT, Hwang CS, Kreiner P, Eadie JL, Clark TW, Alexander CG. "The Prescription Opioid and Heroin Crisis—a Public Health Approach to an Epidemic of Addiction." *Annual Review of Public Health 2015*, Advance Copy (January 12, 2015).

14. Substance Abuse and Mental Health Services Administration, 2005, Medication-Assisted Treatment for Opioid Addiction in Opioid Treatment Programs, Quick Guide for Clinicians Based on TIP-43 (November, 2005).

15. "Opiate Withdrawal," Medline Plus, NIH.gov (December 21, 2017), www.nlm.nih.gov/medlineplus/ency/article/000949.

16. "Opioids," NASADAD v 02 (February 2016), http://nasadad.org/wp-content/uploads/2016/02/Opioids-version-II-Final-2016-1.pdf.

17. "Opioids and the treatment of Chronic Pain: Controversies, Current Status, and Future Directions," Andrew Rosenblum

et al., NCBI (October 2008), http://www.ncbi.nlm.nih.gov/pmc/articles/PMC2711509/.

18. "Prescription Drug Overdose in the United States: Fact Sheet," CDC.gov (October 23, 2017), CDC.gov/homeandrecreationalsafety/overdose/facts.html.

19. "Quick Guide for Clinicians: Medication-Assisted Treatment for Opioid Addiction in Opioid Treatment Programs" (November 2005), https://store.samhsa.gov/product/Medication-Assisted-Treatment-for-Opioid-Addiction-in-Opioid-Treatment-Programs/QGCT43.

20. "The Importance of Medication Assisted Treatment," https://www.shatterproof.org/treatment/Medication-Assisted-Treatment-MAT-for-Opioid-Addiction.

21. "Consensus Statement on the Use of Medications in Treatment of Substance Use Disorders," NASADAD (January 2013), http://nasadad.wpengine.com/wp-content/uploads/2011/06/NASADAD-Statement-on-MAT.pdf.

22. "The Economic Burden of Prescription Opioid Overdose, Abuse, and Dependence in the United States," *Medical Care: Official Journal of the Medical Care Section, American Public Health Association*, v. 54, issue 10 (October 2016), p. 901-906.

23. Tom Hill, Vice President of Addiction and Recovery, National Council for Behavioral Health, Phone Interview, (November 7, 2017).

A Bad Night

— Barbara Lodge —

"Are these okay?" My son motions towards the red plastic bowl containing a few pieces of torn sourdough bread. "Too big?"

"Zach, they're fine. Any way you tear them is fine; they're just for stuffing."

Still, he hesitates, and as I sit next to him at the table and watch him labor over symmetrical circles or squares, I sense that his post-rehab confidence is tender and new, just being born. His fresh skin and crystalline blue eyes suggest that ten months clean and sober have agreed with him. I hope he's agreed with them; we haven't seen each other much in the few weeks since he found work, moved out of sober living, and into his own apartment.

Tonight I want to take hold of his hands and ease his mind of any uncertainty or discomfort. I want to reassure him that I'm proud of his new life, he's doing a fine job with the bread, and all he needs to do is stay away from drugs and good things will begin again.

I grab an unopened loaf and start haphazardly tearing pieces, hoping he'll notice my nonchalance. "How have you been, Zach? You're looking great!"

"I'm good…" But then he says, "Except everyone's over-reacting to what happened. The overdose wasn't a big deal—it was just a bad night."

What? Where is this going? Why now? I stay silent, stunned.

He tells me he's not like those guys in rehab, and he's definitely not an addict. After being sober for almost a year, he has a new plan. "I've decided I won't take pills; I'll just drink and smoke weed. I'll be 'sober enough.'"

Sober enough? Bullshit. After all you've put me through? You almost died, for God's sake. Get out of my house and come back when you're sane. Haven't you learned anything?

But I say nothing. If *I've* learned anything, it's that I don't know anything, especially about what's going on inside of my son. Especially about what underlies his drug use. He is harder on himself than any twenty-one-year-old has a right to be. Although I try, I don't understand how or why he suffers, what his fears are, his insecurities, what lurks in his dark places. I should know those things, but I don't. My yelling at him is nothing more than white noise—frustration at my limitations crashing into his.

So, I steel myself and calmly inquire, "Um Zach? I'm not sure what you're saying." He looks at me, imploring (or is it manipulating?) glistening oceans in his eyes. "Mom, I can't imagine being sober forever."

He's twenty-one and can't fathom a lifetime of abstinence. Drugs and alcohol feel good. He doesn't want to be a drug addict. Who would?

For two decades, I've been sheltering him from the storms of his father's addiction, our divorce, life's tragedies. I built a lifeboat of the finest wood and thought we were happily bobbing along. I made things easy, loving him in the well-intentioned yet materialistic way my mother loved me, shielding him from even his own mistakes; rewarding him with "things" for the least amount of effort. Denying, denying, denying the hard stuff.

We watch an episode of *Modern Family* as we chip away at the eight loaves of bread. "Mom, you sure this size is okay?"

Since his overdose, since he was found in a hotel room barely conscious foaming-at-the-mouth, since his music partner called 911 and the ambulance came and took him to the hospital, since he was given back to us whole, I've tried not to blame myself for missing something, for falling short as a mother. For loving too hard; for loving too soft. In theory, I accept the truth of his addiction and of my own powerlessness over his choices, but in practice, I still torment myself with what I could have done, or not done, that may have kept him safe.

In our family, denial is a force of nature.

When the show ends and the loaves are done, he stands to leave. *So soon? Weren't we having fun? Please don't go.* We hug, and while I cover the bowls with Happy Thanksgiving kitchen towels letting the pieces harden overnight, I call out, "I'm excited for tomorrow."

"Me too, love you Mom, see you at two p.m."

But on Thanksgiving Day, as scents of turkey and stuffing fill the house, two p.m. turns to three p.m., then four p.m., five p.m., then dinnertime, and he hasn't arrived. I call his dad who tells me, "Don't worry; he probably had something better to do." But I know my son. He wouldn't miss this holiday. My family sits down to eat and be thankful while I quickly check outside just one more time. Petty conversations, discussions of world events, and a few gushes that "this turkey is the best you've ever made" do nothing to calm my nerves because something is very wrong with this picture. I look at my partner wide-eyed with terror, my hands shaking, losing their fragile grasp on serenity.

"Wait it out. He's fine," she says to me under her breath.

Wait it out?

Over the past two years while Zach's been in-and-out and in-and-out of treatment, we've lost nine young friends to opiate overdoses. One after another, like falling dominos, kids are dying. The parents, good parents; the kids, sensitive and loving. Like me, like Zach. There's a war going on and it has invaded my small country.

Sometimes I write down their names just to look at them and remember: No one is safe. No one is immune. Lives are lost in a millisecond. These are our children.

Catherine — stepped in front of a moving train after being kicked out of sober living

Thomas — fatal overdose the day he got home from rehab

Kevin — brain death from overdose while living in sober living

Melanie — fatal overdose between appointments as a personal trainer

Christian — fatal overdose the day he got home from rehab

Matthew — fatal overdose while house sitting

James — fatal overdose while in sober living

Toby — fatal overdose

Lyle — fatal overdose

I eat my dinner on autopilot, choking down heaping fork-fuls so my plate will empty and we can move on. I skip the stuffing and can't taste the turkey, creamed spinach, or even the honey-baked ham. Racing thoughts hijack my senses: Don't catastrophize, smile every now and then, stay calm for your family, BUT what if, what if, what if he's in a hospital somewhere scared and alone, or worse blue and stiff and… gone…like the others?

Norcos. Oxys. Percs. Vikes. They're everywhere. Pouring from the sky like sheets of steady rain. What will become of him?

Finally dinner ends—empty plates, full stomachs, and still, his vacant chair beside me.

Call the hospitals, call the police, call his friends. Find him!

My partner says, "I think it's time. We should start with his apar–" I rise from the table and grab my keys. Careening down Wilshire Blvd, I repeat, a robot on tilt, "Please make him okay. Please make him okay. Please make him okay…"

The trip is a blur until I stand outside of the locked door of his security building. I frantically buzz residents' buzzers from A to Z and of course no one's there because it's Thanks-giving and they're home with their families. There's no way to get in and I cross the street to be on the same side as the fire station—to be near those who save lives. I sit on the sidewalk rocking back and forth, wishing I knew how to pray. The cement is cool and my head throbs—fear and powerlessness pounding into my skin. As if watching a scene from a movie, I watch my partner follow someone into the building.

I don't go, petrified of what she may find.

She calls my cell—"He's here. He's okay. He was sleeping." And I crack wide open, dropping my phone on the ground and howling up to the sky like a wounded animal, "Thank yooou, thank yooou, thank yooou." Suddenly I'm kicking the goddamn security door because I need to hold him NOW, feel his heart beat, hear his breath, make sure she's right. "Someone help me! Open this goddamn door," I scream to no one and everyone. I'm feral, sobbing, kicking, pounding. Breaking the skin. She opens the door. A gust of cool air. I push inside.

He's sitting on the couch, hanging his head, repentant, self-loathing. "I'm sorry, Mom. I really messed up."

"Yeah, you did, Zach." And as my beautiful boy stands to face me, anger and blame dissolve into the warmth of his aliveness. His heart beats into my chest as my fears and tears saturate his shirt. Yes, yes, he's here, right here. My son is alive; many other parents can't say that.

This is the same scared boy who, seemingly lifetimes ago, stood in the pelting rain behind the preschool gate red face crumpled, lips tight, holding in terrified screams. Brimming with blue water, his stormy eyes begged, "Mommmmyyyy! No, don't go." And I left because they told me to. But when I picked him up, fraught with guilt and remorse, I pinky-swore that I'd always, always, always, always come back and keep him safe and warm and dry.

I didn't know then that my promise couldn't be kept. I didn't know then that Zach was to become his own storm, hurtling himself every which way in order to make us proud, get good grades, finish what he starts; crashing against his learning disabilities; bashing his body with pills, alcohol, weed, pills, alcohol, weed; battering his soul with lost jobs, lost opportunities, lost trust, with lies and deceit and shame; pushing himself towards, then away from his loving family; and finally, yanking himself so close to the precipice that complete self-destruction lay only a breath away.

Trying to protect him from himself is like trying to protect atmosphere from weather.

"Mom, I'm so sorry. I am so stupid. I had some really strong weed last night. I didn't know how it would affect me."

My hands press harder onto his back as he heaves waves of shame and regret. I shed my own tears too—each one a reminder that I don't believe him and I can't save him. In this moment of clarity, this miniscule moment connecting earth and sky, only one thing matters. Love. Love for my son in all his complexities. Love for my son, and for myself—whether he's using or not. And a new feeling borne of compassion, for both of us, enters the room.

I continue to hug him and tell him I love him and yes he majorly screwed up, and yes he made a mess of Thanksgiving for everyone, and his grandmother was so worried, and we all were a wreck, and this is the kind of shit that happens when you do drugs…but still, "I love you more than words can say."

"Mom. I promise this will never happen again." I know he means it, from his heart he means it. Yet I feel a pang of truth and terror that despite his best intentions, this probably *will* happen again.

We're in the eye of the storm. All the more reason to be kind. All the more reason to love, right here, right now.

We sit on the couch where he, again, hangs his head. My heart breaks a little more for his pain and confusion. Our pain and confusion. My son has a disease. Its symptoms include bad choices, irresponsible behavior, self-aggrandizement, self-loathing. If only I could inspire confidence that would seep through his skin, if only he could see his worthiness rather than his failures and setbacks, if only he could internalize the words of Rumi that I've printed and hung above my desk:

Do you know what you are?
You are a manuscript of a divine letter.
You are a mirror reflecting a noble face.
This universe is not outside of you.
Look inside yourself;
everything that you want,
you are already that.

If only I could, too.

❧

"A Bad Night" was previously published in *Voices on Addiction* on The Rumpus.net

Barbara Straus Lodge is a native Angeleno who earned a B.A. in English from UCLA and a Juris Doctor from Pepperdine University School of Law. She is a graduate of the UCLA Creative Nonfiction Writer's Program and her personal essays, mostly about her family's struggles with addiction, have appeared in *Parabola Magazine, The Rumpus Voices on Addiction, Chicken Soup for the Soul, Random Acts of Kindness, The Good Men Project, New York Times, Motherlode Blog,* the *LA Affairs* section of the *Los Angeles Times,* and a variety of anthologies. Ms. Lodge was also a 2017 guest blogger for Speakers for Change and Facing Addiction.

Ms. Lodge teaches writing to incarcerated young girls through WriteGirl, a Los Angeles based mentoring program, and is the founder of TruthTalks™ workshops which offer hope to parents of young adults struggling with addiction. In TruthTalks™ workshops, parents of active addicts have the opportunity to have a dialogue with kids who've found solid recovery. These dialogues with those kids who've "been there" offer rare insight into their motivations and experiences. As a result, parents often de-objectify their addict sons or daughters and begin to see their struggles with new eyes. There is no room for stigma or judgment. The act of talking and listening to kids in recovery opens doors into a new space where parents can connect with their own children through compassion, empathy, and love. Ms. Lodge lives in Los Angeles and has two amazing young adult children.

Oxy

— Tom Pescatore —

frame by frame

your life escapes me

little white pill

many mashed words in a
mixer like mom's 1950
powder blue or green
whatever my mind
sticks to whatever
memory pops out

whatever color smells right

like flour
wisps in sunlit circles
and by the time I write this
I am 30 years old
confined to my bed

in pain

higher still

too weak to resist the next four hours

&

Tom Pescatore can sometimes be seen wandering along the Walt Whitman Bridge or down the sidewalks of Philadelphia's old Skid Row. He might leave a poem or two behind to mark his trail. He claims ownership of a poetry blog: amagicalmistake.blogspot.com. His first poetry collection, *Go On, Breathe Freely!* is out now from Chatter House Press.

Alex's Teeth

(Spiraling Abecedarian)

— Susan Vespoli —

Alex's	baby
bottom	choppers
crept up like	darts.
Duo of	early pearls
emerging	front row
finial twins	grinners
grinders	happy sprouts
held	in mouth like
innocence	jiggled loose, lost,
jammed beneath pillow.	Kid notes
kissed up to tooth fairy	"Leave cash, please.
Lots." The	mom
(me)	never said
"No"	or maybe
only rarely.	Put five bucks under his
pillow, smiled	quietly smoothed
quilt. No sign of	rotting then. Cavity free.
Really	straight
sans orthodontia.	Teeth
to die for eventually	under siege. Addiction is
ugly. I can't watch them	vanquished,
vanishing into	white powder,
wasting gray.	Xed out by OxyContin

Rx. Then junk.
him dissolve,
zilch.

Ya. I can't watch
zero each enamel bead into
Zot.

&

Susan Vespoli lives in Phoenix, Arizona. She received her MFA in 2010 from Antioch University Los Angeles. Her poetry and prose have been published in a variety of spots including *New Verse News, Mom Egg Review, South85 Journal, Writing Bloody,* and *Role Reboot.* Her second chapbook, entitled *I Come from a Line of Women,* will be published by dancing girl press in 2018.

Heroin Addiction: News From the Happy Valley

— Abigail Warren —

Down the road from my house, about a five-minute walk, my street leads into the "Meadows." The Meadows is fertile farmland bordering the Connecticut River that snakes through the valley. It's a great place to walk the dog, bike, run, or go birding. Acres upon acres of feed corn and rye sometimes fill the open fields. When there are heavy rains, everything is underwater. Last summer I saw rows of rotting zucchini.

It's not unusual to see two or three tents tucked in the woods throughout the summer; homeless people make the Meadows their home in the warmer months. I was surprised to see a tent still standing this past November, into the beginning of December. It was way too cold to be living in a tent. Temperatures had dropped into the twenties for several nights. Puddles were icing over, and the river was running cold and steady with heavy rains.

A week later the police found a dead body in one of the tents. A young boy, James, twenty-four years old. Northampton is a small town; our newspaper is thin with news—mostly AP wires—and the front page is just like a good, old-fashioned local newspaper: featuring local fundraisers, news about the high school football team, the local mayor's latest announcements, and news from the local colleges, too.

41

I knew the boy's death would come out over the next few days—something like that doesn't happen here in the valley without it making the front page: a young man found dead in a tent in the Meadows section of town. Police said no foul play was suspected.

That's when I knew—another heroin overdose, another young person dead from drugs.

I thought a few days will slip by and another silent death will be filed away. And some parents somewhere in town, some brothers or sisters, maybe grandparents will spend a lifetime grieving for this lost child.

The story did unravel over the course of the following weeks. A story that our little town won't call an "epidemic" even though the governor knows that is exactly what it is. No one here in "Happy Valley" has had the courage to say what our neighboring Vermont's Governor Shumlin called, "a full-blown heroin crisis."

I was glad when a week later someone in the family came forth and told the boy's story: his struggle with addiction, arrests, courts, jail time, rehab, and the numerous attempts by his family to save this child's life. I say child because when I think of myself at twenty-four, I was still pretty innocent, still ignorant when it came to being responsible and taking risks. One of the local judges even piped in about how the courthouse was trying to deal with the issue of addiction that he witnessed daily in the justice system. But the dead boy's sister talked about how she had tried to get counseling for her brother, but had been told that counseling was "not allowed" while one was in jail. The family tried to get long-

42

term rehab, but that, too, was unavailable. Trying to get any help from a community that was keeping eerily quiet about heroin use and heroin deaths here in what is commonly referred to as Happy Valley.

The Pioneer Valley is made up of three counties: Hampden, Hampshire, and Franklin counties (with Franklin having the distinction of being the second-poorest county in the state). Within a five-month span in 2016, there were over one hundred heroin-related deaths. In the last two years, there have been over two hundred deaths in the three counties that make up the Pioneer Valley.

A local attorney, a friend of mine, remembers back in the '80s when he—and others at the courthouse—snorted cocaine in the courthouse bathrooms. He said it was rampant then. But, he says, "We grew up." I'm not interested in outing the local authorities that have indulged in drug use, but I do find it painfully frustrating to deal with the hypocrisy of substance abuse—hypocrisy within the medical community, the justice system, and even in our Happy Valley neighborhoods.

Northampton is famous for its progressive politics. If there's an *anti-* anything, Northampton has signed the petition, organized the march, and hung up the banner. I think it's safe to say that much of this is due to a town influenced by a well-educated, academic population and the '60s generation that demographically changed the course of history. This was the generation that coined the phrase "sex, drugs, and rock n' roll." This was—and is—a generation that liked to get high.

I wonder if it's going to take the death of someone important in town for people to march, to take to the streets, and to organize like they did when the local elementary school needed a playground, or when the local cancer support group needed funds. It's easy to open our hearts for those who suffer from cancer, as well as those who have Type 2 diabetes or heart disease. We have races, fundraisers, and organizations to give money to support research for these diseases—even though these illnesses can be caused by personal habits. No illness should be a source of shame. This shame gets in the way of taking care of those who suffer. We are asking all the wrong questions. Why are we, as a society, so lonely, so isolated, so yearning to feel any other way than the way we do when we are not eating our way out of pain, smoking our way out of anxiety, shopping our way out of loneliness, or bullying our way for power to hide our own sense of perceived inadequacies?

But no one says to the heart attack victim's family, "What a waste. If only he could have made better choices about the food he ate." No one says to the diabetic (or in the commercials selling drugs to treat it), "Your over-indulgence in food and your failure to exercise is costing taxpayers a good deal of money." No one ever has to serve eighteen months in jail for spending obscene amounts of money at the mall because shopping feeds some sort of emptiness in their lives. For some illnesses, the shame is unspoken, silenced, or medicated.

It is very easy to become addicted to heroin—just as easy, in fact, as to become addicted to alcohol, food, consumerism, money or power. Heroin makes you feel good and helps you find peace. Why are we so afraid to say that? Who doesn't open a wine bottle, pour a martini, light a joint, smoke a cigarette, buy something new but unneeded? We all do because it makes us feel a little better for a little while.

Undoubtedly some addictions are worse than others. Some addictions kill very quickly, some are illegal, some are not. Most are horrifically difficult to deal with, to acknowledge to your family and your friends, and most carry this added burden of shame. Behind every addiction is someone in pain, someone with a mother, sister, or grandchild, and someone with a story to tell.

I know this.

I have been to three funerals in the last two years. My dear friends buried their twenty-two-year-old granddaughter, Ashley. I write that name out so that you can imagine her; see her as someone who suffered, who struggled, who died, someone whose needs were unmet by our health care community, our justice system, or our neighborhoods.

And I buried my niece, Sophie. She was twenty-five. She never hurt anyone but herself and made poor choices while struggling with impulsive behavior—as we all do in different ways.

Let us address heroin addiction and those who suffer—let us find help for them—help from the medical community and the justice system. And when it comes time to bury another human being who has died of a heroin overdose, let us mourn an unfinished life, for the death of one diminishes us all.

(Statistics for this article were taken from the *Daily Hampshire Gazette* and the *Greenfield Recorder*, and local channel 22 News, and MA Dept. Of Health)

❧

Abigail Warren lives in Northampton, Massachusetts, and teaches writing, literature, and poetry at Cambridge College. Her work has appeared, or is forthcoming, in print and on-line, in *Hawai'i Review, Tin House, Monarch Review*, Ducts. org, *Brink Magazine, Gemini Magazine, Sanskrit, Emerson Review, The Delmarva Review, Serving House Journal,* and other places. Her essays have appeared in *SALON, Northampton Media,* and the *Huffington Post.* Her book, *Air Breathing Life* (Finishing Line Press, 2017) is available.

Sophie

— Abigail Warren —

*What we are doing hasn't worked, it's never going to work, and we need to change our whole approach. Tinkering around the edges isn't going to make a differen*ce.

– Alex Wodak, MD Director, Alcohol and Drug Services
(from *In The Realm Of Hungry Ghosts* by Gabor Matte)

They brought Sophie into the courtroom with shackles on her ankles and handcuffs on her wrists. She was there, in court, for not showing up for a probation appointment. (She had been recently released from a ten-day drug detox center, but was on probation for traffic violations.) I sat a few rows back. She was turning her neck, searching for me. I walked up to her and tapped her on the shoulder and smiled. A courtroom guard walked over to me and said, aggressively, "Get away from her. She is still in custody."

I returned to my seat.

She turned around again.

I blew her a kiss.

She mouthed silently, *I love you.*

That was the last day of Sophie's life.

After the courthouse, I took her out for coffee and to buy some cigarettes. Sophie was so happy to be out of jail. One week. The probation officer said that one week in jail would "teach her a lesson."

Sophie called Jennifer, her mom, as soon as we got in the car. She knew her mom was worried, and Sophie needed to hear her mother's voice—the way children need to hear a mother's voice when they are frightened. Sophie loved to talk—she told me all about the women she met in jail, some of whom were serving two-year sentences, and how glad she was that she only had to be there for one week. One woman had asked Sophie for some writing paper from her notebook so that she could write to her three children. They sell paper at the jail for a price, and, lacking the funds, this woman had been unable to write to her children since being locked up. Sophie gave her the entire notebook.

Sophie told me that all the Puerto Rican girls had wanted to braid her hair. Sophie had long, golden brown, curly hair that fell down half her back, and green eyes. She usually kept it swirled in a bunch of curls on top of her head, but that day she had multiple braids pulled up on top—courtesy of the Puerto Rican inmates.

I was with my sister the day Sophie was born, along with my twelve-year-old son, Jake. It was always the four of us. And every year we went to Cape Cod to celebrate Sophie's birthday: August 8, 1988. She loved to tell everyone that: 8-8-88. The summer she turned ten, she convinced me to join her in a small rubber boat. I agreed and Sophie took me fifteen feet from the shore and proceeded to rock the boat until we both tipped out, howling with laughter, into the cold waters off the Cape. She sang "Red Is the Rose" at Jake's wedding, and when he became a father, she took care of his daughter, Emeline, for the first six months of her life.

Sophie had an ear for music and mimicry; she was a gifted musician who could listen to someone speak and, within minutes, imitate their accent and intonation perfectly.

And so Sophie told me her stories of her week in jail. I heard them all—she had every voice, every story, including guards (who were, apparently, either worn and bitter about their work or inclined to believe that people who end up in jail don't deserve to be treated like human beings). We sat in my car in the driveway of her mother's apartment building—a two-bedroom they had been sharing for the last few months as Sophie was trying to get her life back on track.

Sophie told me about the bad choices she had made over the last few years, about the guys she had dated. She had just ended a relationship with Sean, a troubled young man; she admitted they weren't good for each other.

But then she added, "But you know, Sean deserves to be loved, too."

"Yes he does," I said. "But maybe not by you."

She agreed. But that was Sophie—always a soft spot for the "throwaways," the forgotten, the outsiders. Perhaps she saw herself as an outsider, having spent twenty-five years of her life negotiating a relationship with an absent father.

We talked about what she would do with her day—she was planning to see her dog and take him for a nice, long walk, call her boss about painting the next day, get her life organized again.

I had to leave, to get ready to go to my own job.

I asked her if she had any drugs upstairs; no, she said.

I reached over and hugged her and gave her a kiss, told

her I loved her.

I said, "You know, I'll never give up on you."

She said, "You promise?"

"Yes."

"I love you too, Ab," she said.

Our last words.

Sophie got out of the car and climbed the stairs to the apartment.

I saw her seven hours later on a bed in the hospital emergency room. Sophie was dead; her lifeless body on a gurney; an intubator down her throat. Her mother, my sister, curled up in a ball on the floor, rocking back and forth, crying *no, no, no, no.*

I asked the nurse to remove the tube from Sophie's mouth. She refused, and told me that she couldn't be touched until a coroner investigated.

My sister said, "Will you forgive me if I kill myself?"

I said, "Yes, but please don't do that."

My doctor, a week later, told me that Sophie must have felt an immense shame from her experience in jail.

I painfully agreed.

While heroin addicts are incarcerated, their bodies develop an intolerance to the drug. A dose that once created their high, or relieved them of their pain, could, after release, kill them. According the National Institute for Health, incidences of fatal overdoses greatly increase after incarceration.

I wish I had known that.

I wish that the probation officer who had wanted to teach Sophie a lesson had said, "Don't leave her alone those first few days or weeks. She will be wracked by shame."

I have asked myself a million questions about that day, and I have a million regrets, a million explanations, but none will bring my Sophie back. It's difficult, too, to ask myself how this vibrant, beautiful young woman got addicted to heroin. Where do I begin to answer that question? And what would be the point?

Our thoughts and judgments about heroin addicts are shaped by our limited experiences of understanding the pain and struggle of addiction, and the particular grief and pain of these human beings. No one wants to become a heroin addict. But we must let go of judging how people attempt to relieve their pain, and find compassion and answers that will help them.

Grade School Photo

— Edison Jennings —

Well-groomed and wearing Sunday clothes,
the background draped in royal blue,
he did as he was told to do:
he sat and smiled and held the pose.

His mother bought the portrait size,
and keeps it framed upon a shelf,
a memory of his younger self
before the needle sucked him dry

and left him shrunken, out of hope,
in a basement with a toppled chair,
feet six inches in the air,
hanging from a knotted rope.

❧

Edison Jennings is a public school tutor living in the southwestern Appalachian region of Virginia. His poetry has appeared in several journals and anthologies. His chapbook, *Reckoning*, is available at Jacar Press.

Suburbia's Downfall

— Sarah Ghoshal —

My teenage years were idyllic. I lived in a suburban neighborhood surrounded by woods. Kids rode their bikes and went home for dinner when the sun began to set. My family was blue collar, middle class. We didn't have fancy cars or European vacations; instead, my parents drove mid-priced American cars and took us on road trips to places like Yellowstone National Park where my dad wanted to go fishing. The adults in my family all smoked cigarettes. As teenagers, we used to sneak sips from our parents' liquor bottles and drop Jolly Ranchers into Zimas while sitting on an old mattress we moved into the woods for just that purpose. We had goals but no one ever talked about them. We went to D.A.R.E. workshops in school and hard-core drugs—heroin, cocaine—seemed far away and dangerous. We were happy being us.

Now, as I near forty, I have lost four good friends to overdoses in the past three years. Somehow, smoking pot while watching Yankee games turned into taking pills and later, snorting heroin when the pills were unavailable. I never did this personally. I grew up to be a college professor and because of this, I removed myself from their blue collar world to concentrate on my studies. I wasn't around as much, and I think my friends thought they were hiding these addictions from me. But I knew. I feared what might happen and to my ultimate regret, I never did anything, never said anything, because I never saw it coming. I just stuck my head in the sand and hoped everyone would move on. Some of us never got the chance.

The deaths were hard. They still are. The first three floored me, floored my entire group of friends. People said things like, "How did it get so bad?" and "Why didn't we know?" But we all knew. We knew, but because it seemed so cliché to worry about it, to suggest rehab, we just went on with our own lives, selfishly living in our suburban bubble.

We wore black. We cried over picture collages of our oldest friends as they lay in coffins, bloated and made-up versions of themselves. And then, one of my oldest friends, Kevin, died on a Saturday night. I can't remember what I said in response to the phone call. I can't remember anything but the numbness. Kevin was my friend. Just two weeks earlier, he had told me, "I won't turn out like that. Don't worry about me. I'm fine." He said this to my face and I believed him.

What I realize now is that you cannot believe an addict. After he died, our circle of friends fell apart as so many do. We paid tribute to him but then we moved on, hopeful that this would be the end of it, that we wouldn't lose anyone else, that those who were still struggling with addiction secretly might use four funerals to pull themselves out of it. If you think that heroin doesn't touch suburbia, you're wrong. If you think that someone who has told you he's okay is telling the truth, you're wrong. If you think that life in blue-collar, middle-class New Jersey is the kind of life that shields people from the horrors of hard drug use and addiction, you're wrong. It's more terrible than ever and I have the funeral mass cards to prove it.

Before an addict makes the decision to get help, they usually push everyone away and it is easier to say that you have done all you could to help them and then move on with your life. It's easier to say that prescription drugs are no big deal, that your friends would never stick needles in their arms. Just remember, there is more than one way to lose control.

I have kids. I have had to create a distance from that group of people for them, no matter how difficult it was for me to do this. So many of my friends could have—and have—died. I will have to live with this fact forever. In my dreams, I see their faces in different phases of our lives—in the woods as teenagers, on a tropical cruise in our early twenties, drinking tequila and dancing as if our thirties would never happen, smoking cigarettes in the old, orange chairs in the garage, watching Derek Jeter play his last game as a New York Yankee.

All of this is to say that if you think this can't happen to *your* people, you're wrong. *Say* something, *do* something, before it's too late. I'll never snatch Kevin's Red Sox hat off his head again, never listen to him sing a Billy Joel song off-key, never walk our dogs through the swamps and woods behind our neighborhood. Kevin is gone, as are Keith, Dennis, and Tom. But it's not too late for the people you love. Don't make the mistake of thinking suburbia is exempt. Act now.

∂

Sarah Ghoshal is a writer, professor, mommy, wife, feminist, binder, runner, and persister. Her work can be found in *Reunion: The Dallas Review, Cream City Review, The Moon Magazine*, and *Mom Egg Review*, among others. She is a Best of the Net nominee and has two chapbooks, *Changing the Grid* and *The Pine Tree Experiment*. She lives in New Jersey.

Apology to a Heroin Addict

— Sarah Ghoshal —

It's just that I couldn't find
the time to jump the fence
behind my parents' house
and slide open the sliding
door at your parents' house
and tell you that I knew
you were full of shit

and that we all knew,
you fucker, we all
knew you were hitting
it up up there but we
just didn't have the time
to follow you home

and if fiction wasn't
fiction the me from now
could let the you from
then know that after
your funeral it would
truly fall apart

and my brother would
spiral and we would
fight like children,
our friends spreading
far like a giant firework,
gone in one loud instant.

Hart's Cove

— Cynthia McCain —

You tell me that for years
like the moon
you've gone high and low
tide rising and ebbing
like the Pacific at Hart's Cove
that can't be seen from where I walk.

The path goes along the meadow
from under the spruce.
And now I wonder if I have wandered there
alone all this time.

&

Cynthia McCain has published poetry online and in print journals, as well as on drive-in marquees. She has been a forest ecologist, foster care data analyst, fire fighter, waitress, library aid, retail clerk, lab tech, timber marker, dish washer, telephone operator, green house worker, and has worked on an assembly line putting glue in insect traps. She currently lives outside town at the end of a long gravel driveway.

To a Dead Friend

— Brian Koester —

When you chose heroin, you set fire
to an opal and made me watch it crumble to ash

৵

Brian Jerrold Koester holds an MFA from the Bennington Writing Seminars. He is a Best of the Net Anthology nominee. His work has appeared or is forthcoming in *Agni, HeartWood, The Delmarva Review, Right Hand Pointing, Peacock Journal, Poetry Pacific, Louisiana Literature Journal,* and elsewhere. He lives in Lexington, Massachusetts, and has been a freelance cellist.

A Doctor's Perspective

— Ken Benson, DDS —

The death of a loved one is horrendously difficult for any family and losing a parent, child, or sibling to drugs can be even more devastating because of the shame and guilt that is often involved. More and more families are grappling with this particular heartache as overdose deaths involving prescription opioids have increased steadily over the past two decades. Emergency rooms are filled to capacity, treating misuse, abuse, and overdoses of prescription opioids. Although our nation is facing an opioid epidemic of staggering proportions, solutions are finally evolving.

Clearly, the prescription opioid crisis takes root in our healthcare system where too many prescriptions for too many opioids are written for patients. Health care professionals involved with treating acute and chronic pain, many of whom did not receive proper prescription-writing training, often write prescriptions as a matter of simple routine. Without logical, evidence-based prescription methods, health care professionals have, for years, just written standard prescriptions for each patient.

However, in the defense of these healthcare professionals, they are truly swamped with patients and lack the necessary time to give sufficient thought to pain medicine regimens. During health care professionals' training, they are inundated with a high volume of patients and will write prescriptions for patients instead of taking time to educate patients on better alternatives for pain control. Unfortunately, many practicing health care professionals today never received any training regarding opioid prescription writing. "Keep the patient out of pain," is the imperative commonly heard by residents and practicing doctors. The go-to strategy and the quickest method for pain relief is frequently an opioid prescription, even though it is probably not the best option for patient care.

In the 1990s, some opioid pharmaceutical companies exacerbated an already problematic situation by marketing these types of opioid medications to the health care industry. Pharmaceutical representatives left free patient samples at doctors' offices to distribute to any patient in need of pain relief. Many of these opioid pharmaceutical companies followed a practice of granting awards, prizes, and trips to healthcare offices that provided the most business, that dispensed the largest quantities of opioid medications to patients. A very sad business practice, to say the least.

Today, we health care professionals are getting smarter and more responsible about the opioid crisis. First, we have to understand and realize our role in the current epidemic. Pharmaceutical industry, pharmacists, and educators are also becoming more astute regarding opioid prescriptions.

Better and more alternative education is paramount. Understanding addiction treatment and learning how to properly prescribe opioid medications are efforts included in today's education centers. Practicing health care providers in many states are now required to attend yearly pain management and opioid-prescription-writing courses. Taking time with patients to help educate them about alternative pain management and to teach them how to properly use pain medications is essential.

The ongoing education of health care professionals and patients is critical to ending the opioid crisis, as is the support of addiction treatment research. Coordinated care between pain management practices, pharmacies, and patients is a crucial component not only to identify those individuals that are in need of recovery support, but also to help prevent further escalation of this epidemic.

At my practice, we have strict non-opioid medication recommendations for all patients. I still prescribe opioids, but only with a lengthy discussion on how to use and when to use the medicines. My entire staff is involved in this effort. Taking time with patients in all aspects of their care will benefit our patients and promote a broader education within the community as a whole. Together, each of us can provide input, experience, and expertise toward ending the opioid crisis. It is my hope that I am a positive influence for this effort.

❧

Dr. Kenneth Benson is a practicing oral and maxillofacial surgeon in Raleigh, North Carolina. He is the co-author of *Oral and Maxillofacial Surgery Secrets*.

A Visit From Reality

— Jenean McBearty —

Johnny sat at the kitchen table, his eyes fixated on the Creeping Charlie plant, and then on the curtains ruffled by a late-afternoon San Diego breeze. His face was thin again, not puffed up with doughnuts from the many narc-anon meetings he had promised he would attend. He had shaved, but he needed a haircut. Stringy hair looks worse when it's long, especially when a guy is balding on top already. What had he taken, I wondered, Smack or Thorazine?

"Still in school?' he said.

Meaning: It's September. Is there any Pell Grant money left?

"Yeah."

"You still gettin' welfare?"

Meaning: Can you give me money?

"Yeah. We're divorced so…"

"How 'ya feeling?"

Meaning: Do you have any prescription pain medications I can have?

"Fine. It doesn't hurt. I went in, got a spinal, lay down, and snip! Just like that, sterile. No incision. They go through the vagina these days. No scar. Miraculous, huh?"

Now his eyes—red-veined and staring— are fixed on me. Is his nose going to run? Maybe he's done some blow. Then I see a tear. For my soul maybe? I want to swallow, but there's something blocking my throat. It's my heart, I think.

"I guess this means no babies for us," he said.

I'd like to tell him that two kids by two different husbands was enough for me. He was different, husband number three, but ran off before I got pregnant. Not before he gave me trick, syph, and the clap, though. One disease for each year we were together. I pretended there's a lot of dirty toilet seats out there. Thank God for Public Health Departments that test and treat for free. And for churches. I don't need either one anymore. My body and my soul have been battered enough. That lone tear is trekking down his face. I can't let it make me start hoping; God knows that leads to love and wanting a family. I say nothing. I just stare at my pretty new sofa. The first I've ever owned that I bought just because I liked it.

"Good-bye," he said, without a kiss or a wave.

As far as last good-byes go, I suppose it's as good as any.

"Take care of yourself," I said, knowing I might have well said, "Go fly a kite—high."

Meaning: There isn't any hope. So much of life is a lie.

Jenean McBrearty is a graduate of San Diego State University who taught political science and sociology. Her fiction, poetry, and photographs have been published in over a hundred ninety print and on-line journals. She won the Eastern Kentucky English Department Award for Graduate Creative Non-fiction in 2011 and a Silver Pen Award in 2015 for her noir short story, *Red's Not Your Color.*

Chicken

— Susan Vespoli —

"I didn't cause it, can't control it, can't cure it."
~Al-Anon slogan

I tried to write a poem
about how the opioid epidemic
had stolen one of my children,
now an adult,
and how it threatens
like a terrorist
to take another,
about how there's nothing
a mother can do but watch
the way a body thins, how teeth dissolve,
how beings disappear
from behind their own eyes:
the brown or green irises darkening,
the eyeballs resting
in more hollow sockets—
but the words, lines, stanzas
of my poem attempts
were all failures.

So instead I will tell about a golden hen
that appeared in my backyard

like magic
to stand on her four-prong-star feet,
her body an oval covered with feathers
a strawberry blond fluffy as fur
backlit by the sun
when she bent to sip water
from the pale green bowl
I'd placed beneath the Palo Verde tree.
At first she strutted like a little queen
around the center of the grassy expanse
surrounded by oleanders,
sort of haughty, wide-eyed, solo,
but then she began to trust me,
sidling up to my ankles,
saying *bwak, bwak, bwak*
like she had some news to share
and I grew to sort of love her.
Then one day, as it happens,
I looked for her and she was gone.

Susan Vespoli lives in Phoenix, Arizona. She received her MFA in 2010 from Antioch University Los Angeles. Her poetry and prose have been published in a variety of spots including *New Verse News, Mom Egg Review, South85 Journal, Writing Bloody*, and *Role Reboot*. Her second chapbook, entitled *I Come from a Line of Women*, will be published by dancing girl press in 2018.

Intersects

— kerry rawlinson —

He lugs a bucket of water & a squeegee, though he hasn't washed in weeks. His face is beef-jerky brown, creased with celestial bliss. Tooth-less. He bumps between rows of cars as if he's their shepherd. You look through him like a shadow. I focus on brown eyes; wild lashes. When he was a kid he'd roll over & over in fresh-mown grass, tumbling thru leaves, cold-snap-scarred, to lie with his dad on their backs and see the clouds cross over
into shapes.
He was an orphan. A child prodigy. He flunked school. Dirt's his *lingua franca.* He mopped 7/11 toilets each morning with fresh Pine-Sol. He's never been employed. He can't drive. He stole an uncle's Mustang. His bare-black soles ride the sidewalk. He raced pigeons. He raised kids, & never had an affair. His second mistress had red hair. He saw no action.
He's a decorated vet. He's strung-out on amber love-beads. He's certainly on something. Or something slipped   off. He places bets on my resurrection. He says Jesus washed feet. He drank wine with Jesus just last week. He rubs my windshield with that grubby old squeegee, smiling. I hand him a few bucks. He holds his palms up, like he's panned for gold. Then he bumps amongst the cars, fists nudging

metal flanks, sun-kissed as lambs. He's singing. We rumble
like sickly lions, trapped in our shiny black Hummers &
graphite-blue BMW's & frost-white Cadillacs that map
brand-new directions without even stopping.

    Everyone stops
at this intersection. He's smiling. You can't. He sleeps on a
creek-bank in lavender & dew, below ancient starlight,
always awake. I dream. You sleep-walk. We're always at
war. You shoot a look right through him. I fix him in my
sights for as long as I can while you arrange the shadows of
yourself to cross over to the other side of shame. I watch &
watch him cross over   & over,
until I can't see   lashes anymore.

                            ࡥ

Decades ago, autodidact and bloody-minded optimist
Kerry Rawlinson gravitated from sunny Zambian skies to
solid Canadian soil. A long career in Architectural Tech-
nology assisted her family's transitions through the rocky
New World—but Art and Literature's Muses were gagged,
and stuffed in a closet. Fast-forward: they're free! and now
(in-between volunteering duties) Ms. Rawlinson follows

them around the Okanagan, barefoot, her patient husband ensuring she's fed and the grandkids pretending she's not still in pajamas.

Ms. Rawlinson's won contests (such as *Geist*; *Postcards, Poems&Prose*; *FusionArt*) and features lately in *Boned*, *Pedestal*, *Speculative66*; *AntiHeroinChic*; *ReflexFicton*; *pioneertown*; *Minola Review*; *CanadianLiterature*; *AdHocFiction*; *Adirondack Review*; in anthologies such as *Forgotten Women* (Grayson Books) among many others.

Modern Blue

— Jemshed Khan —

When I had a paycheck job,
driving was improvisational
like jazz or cocktails. Mostly,
this meant never crossing
the police presence that hangs
like a blue note over those roads
back and forth from work and home.

The bankers trapped me alive—
bluebloods with insectivorous eyes
and robo-signed appraisals that I sign
on the line. In default: My signature
sticks to me like flypaper. Sheriffs
evict cockroaches like me every day.

Blue as the homeless blues,
I hustle my way streetside,
panhandling while FDA
oils the prescription mill:
Vicodin; Oxycontin; Fentanyl.
I offer poison too. Adderal, crack,
methamphetamine: I can be
any color I want except green.

I shelter in the shelters: City Rescue
Mission, Union Homeless Shelter,
in the eaves of underpasses, in a tent
between the river and railroad tracks.
I bow my head for Salvation Army
breakfast: Blueberry pancakes and syrup.

I earn my junky veins: Shooting-up
in the alley. Jonesing a medical condition.
Blue lights red lights flashing.
Tweaked and itching.
Scabs tracking hungry veins.
Booked and trundled away,
I went cold turkey
to the city jail that day.

≈

Jemshed Khan was born overseas but lives and works in
Kansas and Missouri. Much of his writing deals with ethical
misgivings. He has published around two dozen poems: *Rigorous, Unlikely Stories, Rat's Ass Review*, the chapbook *Nano-Text* (Medusa's Laugh Press, February 2017), *Clockwise Cat, shufPoetry, Pilcrow & Dagger, Heartland: 150 Kansas Poems* and
I-70 Review. He has future work slated for *I-70 Review* (2018)
and *Writers Resist* (2017).

Not Just Pills for Pills

— Anna Schoenbach —

Over the phone, Arlene doesn't sound like a recovering drug addict. Now a sixty-four-year-old mother and grandmother working at an outpatient rehab center, Arlene had what she wryly terms as a "late start" with drugs at nineteen years old. "I was never a drinker," she said, "I just smoked weed."[1] Aside from a very temporary experimentation with cocaine, her drug use didn't become more pronounced than that—until she had a Cesarean section (one of three) and, after the surgery, was prescribed opioid painkillers, an especially potent and risky class of drugs for the pain.[2] "These," she said, dark bitterness lingering in her voice, "were the drugs that finally took me to my knees."

Arlene took the painkillers as prescribed by her doctors, but her body got used to the medications and began producing less of its own pain-relieving chemicals. Soon, she needed a higher dose of painkillers to offset her pain. When the prescription ended and she tried to go without the pills, Arlene found that the pain came right back, stronger than

---

[1] Arlene, speaking in a phone interview on March 12, 2016. Information updated and confirmed December 2017.

[2] The CDC advises caution in prescribing opioids. For pain, other non-opioid options should be considered first. See "CDC Guidelines for Prescribing Opioids for Chronic Pain," United States 2016 (Dowell et al.), Published March 15, 2016, *Journal of the American Medical Association*. Also see "Opioids" – National State Alcohol and Drug Abuse Directors, February 2016 v 02.

ever—along with vomiting, nausea, chills, and fatigue.[3] Eventually, taking the drug started to be about delaying the feelings of sickness and misery for a little bit longer, more than anything else. "I couldn't even get out of bed without taking a pill," Arlene said. "It wouldn't make me feel high, just normal."[4]

This situation went on for years. Arlene's children grew up, her life went on, all with this struggle in the background. She did things she wasn't proud of. She stole medicine from family and friends. She suffered. Finally, Arlene grew tired of feeling awful all the time. She went to an outpatient center and stayed there for eight weeks to get clean. There, the staff gave her medicine to help with the cravings and sickness, and guided her through the worst parts of withdrawal. She went to meetings. And with that strong start, with that support, she started on her path to recovery.

Medications to treat opioid addiction include Methadone, Buprenorphine, and Naltrexone. They go right to the opioid receptors in the brain, where the chemical part of the addiction occurs, and block them off, stopping the sickness of withdrawal and easing the cravings for a fix. This helps people with addiction live normal, functional lives and, ultimately, avoid relapse.[5] But medication alone is not, how-

[3] These are common symptoms: See "Opiate Withdrawal," Medline Plus, NIH.gov for more information. https://medlineplus.gov/ency/article/000949.htm.

[4] Many people with opioid use disorders begin to feel this way – the need to use becomes as essential as eating to their brains, and not using feels debilitating, much like starvation or thirst. See reference 2.

[5] Medication has been shown to help avoid relapse and help people with opioid use disorder get on their feet in multiple studies, and this statement is the educated opinion of experts in the field of addiction. See

ever, a silver bullet—Arlene was not, in her own words, "cured." However, she says, medication saved her life.

After she had been in recovery for a while, Arlene thought she was better. She didn't think that she needed the meetings or help anymore. And, for a while, she was, indeed, fine. But then, her son had back surgery and was prescribed Percocet, an opioid pain reliever, to deal with the residual pain. The hospital needed someone to hold his medication for him so that he would be less likely to abuse it himself. As his mother, she figured that the responsibility of keeping track of his pills naturally fell to her. Besides, she was better. She would, she felt, be fine; so, with this logic behind her, she volunteered to hold the medications.

"I just decided, in my head, that it wouldn't be that bad,"[6] she said. "Sure enough, all the people who told me that was a bad idea were completely right." Arlene ended up relapsing on her son's medicine. Her life became a mess as the terrible irony unfolded, and she "escaped" into opioids. She was relatively fortunate: she didn't stray too far from Percocet, her drug of choice, and never fell to street heroin. Her family and job also managed to stay intact. But it was a few years

"Behavioral Health Treatments and Services," Samhsa.gov/treatment for more information. Also supporting this statement are: "Confronting an Epidemic: the Case for Eliminating Barriers to Medication-Assisted Treatment of Heroin and Opioid Addiction," - Legal Action Center (www.lac.org) (March 2015); GA Enos, Report: "Better outcomes for opioid addiction lie in greater access to medication"; "Medication-Assisted Treatment for Opioid Addiction," Center for Substance Abuse Treatment, HHS and SAMHSA, Shatterproof.org and NASADAD's "The Importance of Medication Assisted Treatment," Statement on Medication assisted treatment (MAT) (January 2013).
[6] See first reference.

of this struggle before Arlene returned to treatment to start again.

To stave off withdrawal, she was again given medication, a regular dose of Suboxone—a combination of methadone and naloxone—that she continued to take for almost a decade as she got her life on track. She was fortunate that she found groups that allowed this. Although attitudes around medication are changing, many groups and even medical professionals in the field still consider medication-assisted treatment to be "using one drug to replace another drug." Or, even, still using.

Arlene does not agree. Addiction, she feels, is like any other chronic disease and medication is an essential part of dealing with addiction that should be used more often. At the very least, she says, it saves lives by stopping the cravings and making it less likely that someone will overdose on the drugs. "If Suboxone was more readily available," she said, "there would be thousands and thousands of people who would be alive because of it."[7]

"People don't understand addiction as a brain disease," says Tom Hill, Vice President of Addiction and Recovery at the National Council for Behavioral Health.[8] "A lot of people still think about it as a moral failing, even though we have the science that says that it is a chronic brain disease... It can be treated like other chronic conditions—things that the

---

[7] Arlene, phone interview, March 12, 2016. This was Arlene's own opinion (see first reference) but it is one supported by Behavioral Health Treatments and Services (Samhsa.gov/treatment)'s assessment and agrees with their stance that MAT saves lives.

[8] From a phone interview with Tom Hill, Vice President of Addiction and Recovery, National Council for Behavioral Health, on November 7, 2017.

medication is not a cure for, but you can manage."[9] It is not unheard of for people to be on these medications for the rest of their lives, keeping their addiction at bay. "I've known so many people on medication-assisted treatment that I would definitely consider in recovery," said Tom.

Arlene was happy that medication had been available to her when she needed it. However, Suboxone was not something she wanted to be on forever. She was doing well, but at meetings, she heard people talking about how "free" they felt if they went off the medication. She wanted to see what they meant, but going off Suboxone meant sickness, something she wasn't ready to face for a long time.

"I was on it way too long," she felt, "not for fear of relapsing...but for fear of withdrawal." Arlene said. Eventually, however, after years of being on Suboxone, she worked with medical staff to wean herself off. They helped her deal with the withdrawal symptoms as they arose with other medications and therapies. Between them, her doctor, and her meetings, she was finally able to wean herself completely off Suboxone in May of 2015. "I feel like a different person," she said, "I didn't have to take anything anymore."

"I think," Tom continued, "that as medication-assisted treatment gets more prevalent, people will understand it more—it's out of the shadows, as it were, so more people know people who are on medication." Addiction is also leaving the shadows and being understood as an illness rather

[9] This statement is supported by Kolodny A, et al. 2015, "The Prescription Opioid and Heroin crisis - a Public Health approach to an Epidemic of Addiction." Annual Review of Public Health 2015, Advance Copy (January 12, 2015). The idea of addiction as a chronic brain disease, treatable with medicine, has grown in acceptance in recent years.

than a moral failing, as something to be treated instead of punished. But, Tom asserts once more, it is not enough. "If someone is on medication," he explained, "they still need to be able to talk to a counselor. They need to talk about their underlying issues, their childhood, their past, their family… They need to explore the roots of their addiction." Tom is concerned that people are now starting to see medication as the be-all-end-all of opioid treatment.[10]

Arlene puts it more succinctly. "It's not [just] about the substance," she says. "It's about the feelings…[addiction] is a feeling and thinking disease." She needed the medication, but also the meetings and the support groups. "It's important to stay connected—to pick up the phone and call someone. It's important to stay involved in some way." She hasn't forgotten the lesson of her relapse.

As of December 2017, Arlene is doing well. She is on her second husband, whom she met in recovery, with five children (two from her husband's previous marriage) and a lot of grandkids to spend the holidays with. "It's really a day at a time…an hour at a time…a minute at a time." She says. It has now been eleven years since she's taken an opioid and, sometimes, it can be difficult. She knows she is not cured—only recently, when her best friend passed away and she helped to sort through the things in their house, she saw bottles of pain medicine sitting in the cabinet. "They called my name," she said, "and I had to leave as soon as possible." She doesn't risk a piña-colada at a Bat Mitzvah or a joint with a friend, because she doesn't want that to lead to a slippery

[10] Tom Hill's personal opinion and concern that he shares with other professionals in the field—See source 8 for more information.

slope. "And before you know it," she added, "I'll be looking through medicine cabinets for Percocet." But she remains positive. "It's a victory at a time," she said, and she is confident that she can keep it that way.

She is glad she was in programs and never had to go through recovery by herself, and this, she says, is why she loves her job at an outpatient rehab center so much: "I get to help addicts every day," she says. "I get to help addicts every day." But she will always have a special respect for medication-assisted treatment, and for Suboxone, the pill that helped her.

"I don't think I could have done it without it."

☙

Anna Schoenbach is a freelance writer who writes articles on science, with a smattering of fiction and, recently, a poem published in Kelly Ann Jacobson's *Way to the Heart* anthology. Her writing is born of a desire to peel away the curtain and show people why the world is a fantastic and fascinating place, and life an overwhelming cacophony of beautiful sensation. She hopes that she can capture and share even just a little bit of that feeling through her writing

Screaming Really Loudly into van Gogh's Severed Ear

— Justin Karcher —

I watched him convulse on the steps
Like a dreadlocked fish out of water
His friend was screaming, "He's dying, he's dying!"
I was next door and shirtless and chain smoking
And swiping right on everyone on Tinder
When the paramedics came, he suddenly burst into life
Then he started crying, then he began gagging on violent
   vomit
His stomach turned inside out right in front of me
It smelled like roses and I thought of those Virgin Mary statues
That weep tears of blood
He almost died of a drug overdose
It's a miracle he survived
He didn't want to ride the ambulance alone
But that's what happened
His friend was drunk anyway
When the dust settled and the red lights went out
I got up and stared at the puddle of vomit
I stirred it with a stick like I was a witch stirring some cauldron
Trying to predict the future and it was hypnotizing
Like a star being swallowed up by a black hole
So this is what loneliness looks like, I thought
It will never ever end

Suddenly I heard a ding and so my eyes climbed out of the
    overdose
Cause I knew I got a match on Tinder
And wanted to see who might fix this loneliness
I was unimpressed but would message her the next day
After all, there were van Gogh tattoos bleeding out of her chest
Severed ears and starry nights swirling together like a milkshake
Suddenly a feeling of strangeness washed over me
Like I was shampooing my hair with divine knowledge
And it was seeping through the follicles and into my brain
I saw all the people that could roll around in my bed
Emotional architects with dead eyes feeding me drinks and
    pinpricks
And when you're at a low point in your life this seems alright
But you can't build a skyline out of whiskey dicks
That's no city you wanna live in
Where the buildings don't rise like they should
That's a city of the dead
I looked again at the puddle of vomit, saw my reflection
Saw that the future is messy and turns us all into bitter witches
Brewing lovesick potions and crafting spells with needle
    marks and cat hair
Addicted to the things that go bump in the night

So I put on a shirt and went for a walk
Looking for those things that go bump in the night
Looking for anything really
The night sky was full of curled-up salmon looking to spawn

What the hell, I thought, I'll just go with the flow and try to
    spawn too
The least we can do with our pain
Is to keep splitting it in half until there's nothing left
That's how you defeat loneliness, how you force it into
    hiding   after all
In human bodies nearly two trillion cells divide every day for
    us to survive
Why should hurtfulness or the torment all around us be any
    different?
Just look at me: I was once in love with a heroin addict and
    her ghost is everywhere
So are the ghosts of friends and family who convulsed on steps
Ghosts that didn't make it to the street
Ghosts that didn't make it into the ambulance
Ghosts that didn't split in the nick of time
Ghosts left with the totality of their loneliness
Their wholeness is haunting, all-consuming
They couldn't disconnect from their bad parts

Anyway, as I walked up Grant St trying to split myself in two
I was wondering if we're truly alone in the universe
Well, feels like I have one foot in the tundra and the other in
    the desert
And there's holes in my boots tired of running after anyone
So maybe   but I sure as hell hope not
The badness runs through me like Spanish bulls
Suddenly it was 1:14 a.m. and the start of my sunset split
I lost my stomach on the front steps of the West Side Bazaar

Where five months ago I tried new Burmese dishes
And the food was good
Maybe hunger for newness is the cure to all of this
Down the street I lost my eyes when they were swallowed up
By the electric chair windows of this dingy apartment building
Where I knew the lonely motherfuckers inside were shooting up
Hostels of youthful dementia clogging up city streets
(I still get choked up thinking about her geography)
Maybe being blinded is the only way to make it to the end
    of the desert
I lost my ears as I made my way toward the Niagara River
Cause I blew out my hearing listening to the emptiness all
    around
To the distance between us
Humanity hasn't slept in the same bed for over 200,000 years
The trick I think is to ignore the complaints of mattresses in
    the middle of the night

By night's end I was broken man
I sat on a meteorite by the river's edge
Trying to piece myself together again
Then suddenly as if by witch's magick
I saw my city of whiskey dicks being burned to the ground
Then the river transformed into a hateful cauldron
There were severed ears of ex-lovers floating like ice on the
    current
There were pallbearers locking lips in canoes made from
    family trees
I flicked my blunt into the pagan stew and watched all the

ghosts get high
They swirled heavenward and came together like a storm front
Hauntingly and stubbornly whole
And I felt myself being swallowed up by the democracy of regret

Then suddenly there were these starfish running from the cops
They were armed only with their good parts
They ran straight into the river's harmful bloom
Where, hand-in-hand, they constellated into something to
     live for: each other
Cause I guess when you feel like you're drowning in loneliness
You gotta hang on   for the love of God you just gotta
     hang on

"Screaming Really Loudly into van Gogh's Severed Ear"
first appeared in *Buffalo Rising* and appears in the chapbook
When Severed Ears Sing You Songs.

ॐ

Justin Karcher is a poet and playwright born and raised
in Buffalo, New York. He is the author of *Tailgating at the
Gates of Hell* (Ghost City Press, 2015), the chapbook *When
Severed Ears Sing You Songs* (CWP Collective Press, 2017), and
the micro-chapbook *Just Because You've Been Hospitalized for
Depression Doesn't Mean You're Kanye West* (Ghost City Press,
2017). He is the editor of *Ghost City Review* and co-editor of
the anthology *My Next Heart: New Buffalo Poetry* (BlazeVOX
[books], 2017). He tweets @Justin_Karcher

Soul-Rot

— Nathanael Stolte —

I lost the eulogy
I read at your funeral,
Of the many things
I've not valued enough in my life
To keep track of,
That is one of very few I truly regret.

Not as much as the last time I saw you breathing,
When we argued like brothers.
I don't remember what it was over,
But that's the way it goes sometimes.

You gave the best advice
You never could live.

The pain gets great enough,
One way or another.

It was too much for you.

I forgive you for giving up.

I think of you sometimes,
When I swim in murky waters,

You were too into drowning.

Last autumn I walked by
The old apartment
We called home,
Where we smoked glitter &
Practiced glamour.

Where you invited the crazy in.

Unmolested silence and memories
Float to the surface,
Your frail frame enveloped
In pine and satin
Like a wax museum horror.

Whatever spark that was you left.
I take solace in knowing
The me I am today,
Wouldn't be able to stomach
The me in you.
You were circling the drain.

Smoldering memories corrupted,
Perverted by the choices we made.
You always preferred ugly truth
Tempered with love
Over sugary lies.

I love you dope angel,
I'm glad you're dead.

∂

Nathanael William Stolte is the author of five chapbooks, *A Beggar's Book of Poems* (Last First Press, 2015), *Bumblebee Petting Zoo* (CWP Collective Press, 2015), *Fools' Song* (CWP Collective Press, 2016), *Origami Creature* (Ghost City Press, 2017), and *A Beggar's Prayer Book* (Night Ballet Press, 2017) . This year his poems have appeared in *Guide to Kulture Creative Journal, Rusty Truck, Poems-For-All, The Buffalo News, Le Mot Juste, Foundlings Zine, Iconoclast, 34th Parallel Magazine, Poets Speak Anthology, Punch Drunk Press, My Next Heart: New Buffalo Poetry* and *Mutata Re.* He was voted best poet in Buffalo (Artvoice, 2016). He is a madcap, flower-punk, D.I.Y. Buffalo-bred and corn-fed poet.

Roots of Recovery

— Laura Golden —

It was winter and my first day living on Topsail Beach, North Carolina. A year earlier, I'd quit my corporate job after a decade and spent most of 2016 traveling around Central America, where I started writing a collection of short stories. When I returned after Christmas, I couldn't move back into my own house in Wilmington because it was still rented out, and besides, I had too many friends there, too many distractions. I needed peace and quiet to finish my book, so I headed north to Topsail Island.

Although just a half hour north of Wilmington, Topsail might as well be on another planet, especially the far north end, which is where I wound up. Topsail is one of those long, thin, barrier islands common to North Carolina, with the ocean on one side and the intra-coastal waterway on the other, trying their best to meet. Like most of these islands, Topsail is packed with tourists from Memorial to Labor Day, but deserted the rest of the time. It's twenty-six miles long, and if you're heading to the north end—especially off season—you'd best be sure to bring what you want, because there's nothing to buy once you get there: no grocery stores, no restaurants, no bars, no shops. Just what I was looking for. I had four months at my little beach bungalow before the owners reclaimed it for the summer, a deadline I set to complete my book.

In addition to my corporate job, I was, and still am, a yoga teacher, so after unpacking my bags, I settled in with a cup of herbal tea and did what I always do when I arrive someplace new: checked out the local yoga scene. After a little Internet sleuthing, I discovered the nearest place to take a yoga class was at the Surf City Community Center, a good twenty-minute drive all the way down-island and back over the bridge to the mainland. While I was on the Facebook page, a new event popped up for the area: Roots of Love Yoga Festival. *Where and when is this?* I wondered as I clicked on the pop-up. Surf City, the week before I was due to leave at the end of May.

Impossible to ignore the serendipity, I messaged the event planner, Catherine McDowell. I explained I was a yoga teacher, new to the area, and interested in learning more about the Festival. The next morning, after a lovely yoga class at the community center, I met Catherine for coffee at The Daily Grind in Surf City. It turned out she wasn't just the event planner for the yoga festival; she was a founding member and the director of the organization behind it, Roots of Recovery. Overflowing with enthusiasm, Catherine explained Roots was a local non-profit formed by a group of concerned women, including herself—mothers, daughters, friends, neighbors, professionals, and students—all directly affected by the trauma surrounding substance-use disorder.

The organization is based in Pender County, neighbor to New Hanover County, which is much larger and includes Wilmington, the biggest city in the region. According to a recent health-care information report, Wilmington ranked number one in the entire nation for opioid abuse, two years running.[1] Three other North Carolina cities made the top twenty-five. Another study claims alcohol abuse is the third-leading preventable cause of death in the state.[2] The statistics are plentiful and staggering. Substance abuse and dependency in the region—in the nation—are now pervasive and ubiquitous; solutions are not. Roots of Recovery is a grassroots effort that arose from this dearth.

In the coffee shop that day, Catherine asked me, "How many beds do you think there are in Pender County for a person seeking treatment?" I had no idea. "Zero!" she shouted, making the shape with her fingers, and then spit out similar numbers for the surrounding counties. "The problem is even worse for women," she explained, "especially women with children." Mothers don't seek treatment because they're afraid their children will be taken away from them—which happens all the time—or they can't afford daycare, or lack a family support system, or earn just enough to stay above the poverty line but not enough to pay for treatment. It is for these women that Roots of Recovery was created.

In addition to identifying this underserved community, Catherine and her organization address another void in substance abuse treatment. Aside from Alcoholics Anonymous (AA) and Narcotics Anonymous (NA), there are no relapse prevention services in the area, which are the other half of the equation for recovery. Without viable support systems after treatment, substance abusers almost inevitably relapse.

[1] Christopher Whaley, *Castlight Health*, "The opioid crisis in America's workforce." (San Francisco: February 2016 and 2017).
[2] NC Division of Public Health and CDC Alcohol Fact Sheets.

But people don't live at AA and NA; once the meeting is over, they're on their own. Roots of Recovery is tackling this issue by creating a sober community where women can live, with their children, after they complete a treatment program. A central tenet of the organization's philosophy is that every woman should receive positive social support, free from fear of becoming homeless or losing her children.

The yoga festival that led me to Catherine turned out to be a fundraiser for Roots of Recovery. By the end of our coffee date, I was on the planning committee, and I've been a volunteer for the organization ever since. That first festival in May 2017 was so successful that we decided to make it an annual event. We raised enough money to purchase land, and as of this writing, just six months later, a cottage development is already in the design phase. It will include a small home for each woman as well as common areas for meals and childcare. Later phases of the project will provide several means for the women to live sustainably: an organic farm, a fishery, and an apiary. In addition to the skills they will learn in these endeavors, the women will be encouraged to complete or further their education, and services such as job training and placement will aid them in integrating back into society in their own time, which is the ultimate goal. Unlike other residency programs, once the women leave, in times of weakness, if they feel the need for community support, they will be welcome to return until the moment passes and they are strong enough to leave again, knowing they can resist any influences to relapse.

Catherine and her co-founders are adamant that the lasting effects and success of Roots of Recovery's program lie in holistic, peer-supported recovery through the benefit of shared experiences. For the past two years, without the land or even a permanent building to use, they have provided services to newcomers. Based on their own personal experiences with substance-use disorder, these pioneering women—trained in a variety of holistic interventions such as massage, yoga, and Reiki—offer their services to newly sober women in order to ease their transition into recovery, addressing the physical, mental, and spiritual ills that accompany long-term abuse of drugs and alcohol.

"It's simple!" Catherine said with her shining smile that day in the café. "We're building a sustainable community for women to achieve long-term sobriety. It will work. I should know: it worked for me."

For more information about Roots of Recovery, please visit their website: www.RootsOfRecovery.org.

Laura Golden is a traveler, sailor, yoga teacher, and writer. Originally from New York, she has lived in Wilmington, North Carolina, for the past ten years. She recently completed a series of short stories inspired by her travels throughout Central America in 2016, one of which was shortlisted for the Doris Betts Fiction Prize. She has published several yoga articles and translation excerpts.

All the Junkies on Carr Avenue

— Damian Rucci —

look a lot like us
in the yellow street lights
that paint
their silhouettes in flickers
skeletons
in dirty denim dance
behind burning red embers
they're dead
before the next needle hits their
flesh
what happened to *what's-his-name?*
Or the one after that
or you
with your baby blue eyes
how did *we* become *this?*
We broke the vows of the block
we would never sniff powder
never chew pills
never charm the veins to the surface
by tying off a band of rubber
a syringe in the arm is death without a certificate

nothing stays the same
children

steal cigarettes
and puke on warm beer
weed smoking beauty queens
trade innocence
for hallway ecstasy
the artists dilute their genius
until their souls
are vacant

we are doomed
to be like our fathers
to be burnouts
who die unknown

we are doomed
to step over the bodies
of our
friends

❧

Damian Rucci is a writer and poet from New Jersey whose work has recently appeared in *Beatdom, Eunoia Review, Indiana Voice Journal*, and basements and coffee shops across the country. He is the author of *The Former Lives of Saints* (2017 EMP with Ezhno Martin), *Tweet* and *Other Poems* (2016 Maverick Duck Press), and *A Symphony of Crows* (2015 Indigent Press). Damian is the founder of the *Poetry in the Port* reading series and poetry editor at *Blue Mountain Review*.

Graveyard

— Will Cordeiro —

I knew the right things to say
to score another hit. I knew
I could always break my face

until my crooked nose stared
straight at me in every mirror.
The ER nurse doing nightshift

looks down at his paperwork.
He keeps punching in data—
the screen keeps spitting *error*.

❧

Will Cordeiro has work appearing or forthcoming in *Best New Poets, Blue Earth Review, Copper Nickel, DIAGRAM, Fourteen Hills, Nashville Review, [PANK], Phoebe, Poetry Northwest, Valparaiso Poetry Review, Zone 3,* and elsewhere. His two chapbooks of prose are "Reveries and Opinions of Mr. Figure" (RDP, 2016) and "Never-never" (White Knuckle, 2017). He lives in Flagstaff, where he teaches in the Honors College at Northern Arizona University.

Deal

— Larry Thacker —

My advantage is your imagination,
getting you to think twice and reply,
"Well, we've got to live here, too, buddy,"
when you're asked why you don't turn
me in, not because you want respect
but because there's true reason for fear.

The great *what if* is the best friend
of the pill dealer. It's what always keeps
mountain mouths shut up. You know

what I'm doing. My neighbors all know.
The law always knows. My parole officer
knows. Hell, my own damn mother's
my best customer. Ain't nobody fooling
nobody on this block, yet nobody's
talking either.
        Still, nothing happens,
huh? And come the first of the month
our cute little street becomes my own
cramped parking lot for three days
while all my friends come around
for their five-minute drive-by visits.
So you all just keep smiling and nodding,

keep mowing and trimming up the yard
every Saturday like we're a normal.

I'm just getting by like everybody else.
Come on over if you need something.

☙

Larry D. Thacker's poetry can be found in over a hundred publications including *The Still Journal, American Journal of Poetry, Poetry South, Spillway, Tower Poetry Society, Mad River Review, The Southern Poetry Anthology, Mojave River Review, Town Creek Poetry, and Appalachian Heritage.* His books include *Mountain Mysteries: The Mystic Traditions of Appalachia* and the poetry books, *Voice Hunting, Memory Train,* and *Drifting in Awe.* Visit his website at: www.larrydthacker.com

Make Green the Lawn

— Luke Muyskens —

The last time I felt that content was the winter before
when I fell asleep at home and woke up in a movie theater
playing *The Secret Life of Pets*. For a while
I couldn't place myself in time or space
and the mischievous parrots and cats were mine.
It felt like pissing in a swimming pool
the borders of my body expanding and blurring.

I was overdosing. The sun was rising
inside my body and I knew I was on too much.

An anti-drug campaign made posters showing
a classroom with an empty seat. My seat
had always felt empty because I was dumb
like a kinked hose. Any words I might've had
were diverted near their source.

There were parts of my life I liked. My cousin
promised a kitten from her cat's litter and I could surf.
Dilaudid warms your blood so you don't need a wetsuit
and Lake Superior's big wheels were the ultimate nod.

I walked down Tower where I once saw teens
mug an overweight girl. I followed them
and bought her phone for forty dollars.

I had two convictions: The existence of a physical hell
and that everything could be improved.
I'd died and undied a few times courtesy of Narcan
and had memories of bondage and abuse from beyond
that heavy analgesic curtain. And in my grimiest circumstances
I did nothing to free myself but made improvements.
Some might have moved to a healthy patch of grass
where I made green the fucking lawn.

I waited to go to hell. My friends were shitheads
and I had no money. I thought of death like a canoe paddle.
It once propelled me to eat and sleep but now I was fucked
beyond measure and no longer paddling. Death was
an ungainly wooden thing that didn't apply.

My guy Ricky rolled up on a bike and fished out the strips
I hadn't puked loose to put under his own tongue.

He wanted help racking meat from Super-One
to sell Flame Nightclub for their meat raffle.
Ricky and I had a million ways to cop. We drove hours
to Thunder Bay and crammed pill bottles into our assholes.

Got some back ribs, a Delmonico, and a few sirloins. All top
shelf, certified Angus. Fifty cents on the dollar. Stickers and
everything.

I walked with the cash back to my apartment
remembering sex. On Christmas I crashed my car
and went clean for a month. After the diarrhea stopped

I slept with a high school senior at the Duluth Family Sauna.
Recalling his breath put a pot of honey in my stomach
which sparked a hunger for fentanyl. I realized
why I hadn't fucked or even masturbated for so long—
it would've been like chewing gum when you're hungry.

I slept through the next day and night. When I peeled
from the couch I found a text from Aunt Erin: got something 4 u

I took a bus into Minnesota and down the shore to Norton Park.
Aunt Erin was a somber lab technician with a pristine home
though her soul was rottener than mine in ways.

Aunt Erin once hired me as a lab assistant.
I learned how to synthesize MDMA, 25CINBOMe, and
fentanyl.
Some have confused my cat-snagged tongue for idiocy
when I've always been good at sawing through a knot
instead of untying. The situation needed greening.
I couldn't shit or eat but getting zoned made my day
obscure and sexy. You know the feeling of scrolling Instagram
and seeing your ex swimming with dolphins in Bali?
That's how I felt sober—there was a beautiful place
with a me-shaped hole.

Aunt Erin offered grapefruit. I begged her to roll me a joint.

Your dad asked about you. Does he think you're in school?
He asked about classes. I should ask, are you back in school?
He wants to help with tuition.

My parents' refusal to pay for rehab was part of a machine
of disagreement. After failing to cure my speechlessness
they gave up on their idiot son. My rich inner life
was never apparent to them. When I did amazing things
like crowdfund rent for an empty storefront to screen skate
videos

they saw adjustments required by stupidity
rather than ingenious modifications to a life
with retaining pond stagnancy.

I opened my palm to Aunt Erin. She pulled a check
from her purse and put it on the table.

You're not really in school. But your dad wants to give you
money, so I guess you deserve some. There's a singles cruise
from Rome to Istanbul. I'm going. There's plenty left to buy
yourself some new speakers or whatever. If you decide to go
back to school, I'll give you a loan.

Painful sweat broke through my skin. Meaningless anger
ricocheted between my ears. I wanted to kick her fucking
head off.
I could see it breaking through the window and rolling
into the yard. That bitch had my funds.

I took her check and walked
through the woods along Kingsbury Creek
through a drainage tunnel
into the Thompson Hill Information Center

where I put in two dollars in the payphone
dialed 911
told the operator I had a shotgun
a duffel bag full of plastic explosives
and four hostages
that I wanted a hundred thousand dollars in cash
delivered to 7524 Coleman Street
that if the money didn't arrive in fifteen minutes
I would start executing hostages
every three minutes
until all were dead.

Over the phone it felt like a game. I was thinking
about the good nod I would have. My voice
describing how I'd shoot some kid in the neck
felt like the voice of someone working for me.
It was easy.

I slipped my last sub film under my tongue
and watched SWAT vans roll up. They swarmed
her house and busted down the door. I later learned they shot
Aunt Erin in the chest with fifteen rubber bullets.
They tossed her in a squad car. I laughed when I saw
the familiar confusion in her eyes
like a low-battery light.

My first pills were benzos pilfered from my mom.
Kids have personalities that bend like plastic.
The xan was not a mood swing—
it was my plastic melting.
My mind had reason to be empty.

The muteness solidifying in me was not a shortcoming
but a side effect. Beyond making my silence justified
analgesics made it good. Dilaudid made clear
I had nothing to say because there was nothing to say.
I was unimpeachable.
The dopamine release was nothing
compared to the contentedness of a lifelong flaw
becoming a characteristic of remarkable beauty.

I'm still chasing reasons for my muteness.
Activities that don't require noise
make my lack of voice okay. There is nothing
that makes it good.

When the cops were gone I pried open the back door
swiped all the cash I could find and left in her car.

Being dumb is like moving a pen in hard circles
and drawing nothing. No
it's like having a broken fuel gauge and never knowing
when you'll grind to a halt. No
it's like watching a friend juice an orange
then peeling yours and finding a stone inside.

I had the sense while crossing into Wisconsin
that life was larger and more intricate than I knew.
I had the feeling of moving outside a map.
I wasn't scared. It felt like exploration.
Like glass tightening when filled with ice water
my body recognized the change.

Ricky had Anexia and wanted to meet at Builder's Saloon.
I texted: fuck yr Anexia. im flush. hook me up with good stuff

I was no longer happy with shit pills. I wanted fentanyl or
heroin.
In the bathroom he unveiled four fresh Dura patches
like a ceremony. The hesitation made me furious.
My body was condensing into a blot of pissy lust.
I cussed him out for wasting time.

I regret being so cruel. I was expressing the inferiority I felt
to people who could speak with ease. I suspected
more of life's map was unfolded to them.

An awful question people ask:
What is your ultimate desire?
I have a quick answer—I'd wish for ease.
Some people navigate life so effortlessly
and my jealousy for them is solar.

Rickey was a friend. One of the few
who wouldn't have sold my brain for a fix.
If I knew this was my last chance to zone with him
I hope I would've been more patient.

I pricked a patch with a box cutter
squeezed a little gel onto aluminum foil
hit that shit with a lighter
and sucked the smoke through a one-hitter.

Junkies are obsessed with the process of

dissolving, plunging, loading, firing.
They talk about the drug in hushed tones.
I could've loaded up in a library bathroom
while talking to my mom on speakerphone
with a slice of pizza in one hand.

As I watched Ricky hit the fent every swollen part of me
returned to its normal size. The anger
that was my chronic companion departed
and I had a distinct feeling that my mother was the president.
I felt like someone close to me held immense power.
That I had an ally in a seat of great importance.
That if I truly fucked up
I would be pardoned.

Once my body adjusted to its new state
I realized the familial power belonged not to my mother
but to fentanyl. The pride of proximity to strength
was incidental heat from the drug's overwhelming flame.

Ricky claimed he couldn't feel anything and spread
a ladybug of gel across his gums. I laughed
and told him he was in for hell.
I assumed Ricky's boldness meant his tolerance was high.

Maybe I would have done things differently
if I'd known. That question can kill you.

I never wanted to see how Ricky would turn out.
His choice was between a life of continuing decomposition
or a buttoned-down life of stepping around ambiguity

for fear of relapse. I never wanted to see Ricky
in either position. For that reason
I was happy to see him die.

We left the bathroom gripped by a thousand orgasms
slumped over the bar and ordered drinks. The craggy woman
tending bar
was acting strange. She moved a few yards away
and watched us in her periphery. When we finished our drinks
Ricky suggested we go watch YouTube videos.
At the door a bouncer blocked our exit.

You boys are going out the back today.

We headed for the back without question. I didn't give a shit
about the bouncer or the bartender. Walking through the bar
I felt like a Roomba sucking cat hair from a living room.
Someone put fifteen bucks of Birdman in the jukebox
and I remember hearing 'What Happened to that Boy'
as we crossed the infinite plane of Builder's Saloon.

A memory pushed into my brain. I was twenty-one
on the Outer Banks of North Carolina
driving my dad's Scion. On impulse
I took it on the beach. The car fought through sand
but near the water it gained traction. I opened up
and tore down the beach for miles.
Waves and sandpipers shredded under my wheels.
Fifty, sixty, seventy, eighty miles per hour.
The noise was terrific. Remembering
I grinned like a magnificent dumbass.

The sun outside the bar blasted my ass off.
By the time my eyes adjusted
I was in handcuffs. Who put them on me?
There was a streak of dark blood
on the asphalt in front of my face.
There were places on my skin that felt cold
and open to the sky and I realized they were wounds.
Ricky was gone. There was a man above me.

Through all of this I felt good. I felt patient
like shit would sort itself out.
All I had to do was breathe and wait.
For this and every instance where trauma
was dampened by chemicals
I am grateful.

In jail I learned Ricky had a huge unpaid bar tab.
The bartender heard my bathroom tirade and found
an opportunity
to rid herself of him. They booked the bastard
for disorderly conduct and he overdosed in a holding cell.
Later his family sued the department and lost.

Escaping a lifetime in prison is too large a feat
to comprehend. I feel luckier to have escaped
the more familiar custody of analgesics.
When I hear about the overdose death of a friend
I am flooded with relief and gratitude
for my body.

I miss fentanyl. Every day

I ache for a patch or a drop to smoke.
I experience fleeting happiness
when I pet a cat or eat smoked salmon
but I feel nothing close to the contentment
of fent or Dilaudid. At no moment
do the scattered pieces of life come together
at no moment does silence feel right
or even acceptable. All sober feelings
are complicated and incomplete.
There's a simplicity to chemicals that I miss like hell.

I read recently of a new drug called Carfentanil
that's 10,000 times more powerful than morphine
and 100 times stronger than fent. It's been surfacing
on the streets of Ohio. Even Narcan
can't stop this one from dropping you.

Sometimes I remember recalling the thrilling beach drive
while floating across the bar to Birdman.
This was my last purely joyful moment.
Compared to the limited emotions of the sober brain
the serenity of analgesics is unlimited. It unfurls
like clouds splitting and spiraling forever.

It is endlessly
ridiculously
green.

‪࿊‬

Luke Muyskens lives in Minneapolis, Minnesota. His poetry and fiction have appeared in a few literary journals, most recently *New American Writing, Hopkins Review, CutBank, Arts & Letters*, and *New Madrid*. He holds an MFA in fiction from Queen's University of Charlotte.

Some Good Has Come of This

— D. Ketchum —

I first tried heroin when I was seventeen years old. I only bought one bag, one hit, but that one bag was all it took; I ended up chasing that high for nearly a decade. Now, over a year and a half into my sobriety, I work as an addiction and recovery coach for a local nonprofit, assisting people who are also suffering from substance use issues. Working with and helping others overcome their addictions has become my passion and my purpose. Had it not been for my long and exhausting love affair with opiates, however, I would have never been able to help make a difference in the lives of the people I have since had the pleasure of working with.

When I look back and reflect on the path that has brought me to where I am today, I can trace everything back to one specific moment in time—the very first time I tried heroin. It was over the summer of 2005, a month before my senior year in high school. Ironically, I never actively sought that particular drug. In fact, all I was looking for that day was a bag of weed for a friend and me to share before we went to the local carnival that night. For us, it was just another excuse to escape the monotony of small-town boredom. When we arrived to pick it up, we ended up hanging out for a while with a couple friends-of-friends whom I'd never met before. The conversation was lively, and eventually they asked, "Do you wanna try some dope?" The answer should have been

No, but as a teenager with no self-respect, an affinity for risky behavior, and a love for just about anything that would get me high, I said *Yes*.

I didn't know it then, but that three-letter response would change my entire life. I often wonder what life would have been like had I said *no*, or had I just not gone there that day to begin with. Immediately after I said yes, however, there was absolutely no regret whatsoever. That first time was beyond amazing—the euphoria, the warmth, and the total inner and outer peace were feelings I didn't even know were humanly possible. This initial high is something the human body can only ever experience once, but it's what all addicts continue to chase from there on out, not realizing that they'll never actually achieve that feeling again.

As a high-schooler with a crappy part-time job in the food-service industry, it was very difficult to keep up with my newly formed habit. Within a couple of weeks I was back in school, shooting up in the bathrooms, and trying to find new and creative ways to afford my dope. Eventually, I turned to pawning off what few material possessions I had and stealing money from my siblings, parents, and friends. This new way of life continued in the months that followed, right up until the day I was scheduled to take my SATs. The night before, I had done my last few bags, naively thinking I could wake up the next day, take my test without using and without issue, and then get hooked up afterwards and continue my weekend as planned. When I woke up however, I ended up going through the worst withdrawal I had yet experienced. I was shaking, cold-sweating, and feverish. My body ached and craved, and the idea of trying to take a test like the SAT in that state was completely out of the question. This was my first wake-up call.

A few months passed without any slip-ups. I had replaced shooting dope with smoking copious amounts of weed as my need to get high was still there. I graduated with average marks in all my classes and just barely passed my SAT. Desperately wanting to start fresh and to distance myself from my past and the people there who looked to be following in my footsteps, when an opportunity arose that would allow me to move out of state, I packed my things and left.

The idea that I could run away from my problems, my past, or the people that I once knew was absurdly foolish. The use of opiates and heroin had only grown in popularity over the years and it felt like all I really did was buy myself a little time before diving head-first back in. This time was different though. Now I was an adult with a decent, paying job and very few bills to pay. On top of that, my connection was a disabled veteran with a never-ending supply of morphine and Oxycodone, who hated the way the pills made him feel—and was all too eager to make a quick buck selling everything he didn't want. In short—I was set.

This relationship lasted for the next six years. After a certain point, it wasn't so much about getting high anymore as it was just getting by. I felt as though I truly couldn't get through the day without having some sort of high to look forward to. The tedium of everyday life, working nine to five without any long-term goals and then coming home to an empty apartment, just reaffirmed that using was the only thing I really had. Unlike when I first began getting high, I had no real reason to stop, and as a result, my addiction only grew stronger.

It wasn't until a few years into my ever-growing morphine addiction, that a friend of mine introduced me to a pill that would bring me to my absolute rock bottom. This particular pill was a forty-milligram Opana, or oxymorphone hydochloride. The high I was able to achieve from doing this was the closest thing I'd ever found to replicating that very first high, all those years ago. Not only that, but unlike the other pills I was popping at the time, these could be crushed up, snorted, or injected for a much bigger rush, a quicker onset, and a stronger high. So now, in addition to taking my daily dose of morphine, I was supplementing that with at least one Opana a day.

Naturally, these numbers quickly multiplied as my tolerance grew. Even with a full-time job to support my habit, I eventually couldn't keep up. I began dealing to a small but loyal group of friends who helped me keep up my habit, while also feeding their own. Still, this wasn't enough. I eventually had to start making difficult decisions on what I was going to put my money toward. My addiction came first and everything else, including food, bills, gas, and other necessities, came second. I started losing everything in my life that I valued most. My friends were the first to go as I was no longer the warm and compassionate person they once knew. The only people who stuck around were the ones who needed me for the pills that I supplied them. Just as I did when I was seventeen, I resorted to pawning, selling, and trading in many of my personal belongings to help supplement my income. Books, video game consoles, stereo equipment, and various other electronics began vanishing from my apartment. I maxed out two credit cards in an effort to pay off various bills while using my paychecks to support my addiction.

My boss began taking note of my sloppy performance. Between the constant tardiness, the weekly call-outs while I tried to deal with the withdrawal, and the increasing regularity with which I was getting caught nodding off at my desk, I knew it wouldn't be long before I was fired. My parents, who lived multiple states away, began catching on simply through our weekly phone conversations. They offered to help, but I knew how heartbroken and disappointed they would be if I were to tell them the full extent to which this addiction had taken over.

Then there was the withdrawal, which only became more and more unbearable as I grew older and as my dependency worsened. Opiate withdrawal is like a more agonizing and painful version of the flu that also affects the user's mental health. Intense body-aches are matched only by the depth of depression and anxiety that come with not having the drug addicts crave. Suicidal and racing thoughts, coupled with hellish hot flashes and cold sweats that would persist for days, soon became all too common for me. As much as I loved the high that the Opana gave me, the lows that were brought by the withdrawal were growing to be unbearable. No matter how much money I happened upon nor how many pills I bought, I would always run out and I would always have to endure the harrowing withdrawal that followed. This realization tortured me and, while obvious to anyone on the outside who happens to be looking in, is not something that most addicts can truly come to terms with.

The final nail in the coffin of my addiction came from my best friend of nearly twenty years. She was the only person who never gave up on me and who, despite still living in my hometown more than eight hundred miles away, checked in on me every week, believed in me unconditionally, and offered her support in any way that she could. I told her that I had finally had enough and wanted to try getting on Suboxone to help manage my cravings and withdrawal symptoms. Taking it would allow me to get some clean time and stability as I began my path to recovery. She immediately sent two hundred dollars via PayPal and made me promise that I would only use that money for the treatment that I so desperately needed. I promised, thanking her profusely and vowing to pay her back once I could afford to.

A couple of weeks later, I received a call informing me that my dear friend had passed away from a complication between two of the medications she had been prescribed.

I was heartbroken and devastated. My absolute best and only true friend in the world was now gone forever. I would never again get the chance to speak with her, ask her for advice, or fulfill my promise in paying her back the money she had just lent me. When she passed, I was only a week or two into my sobriety. The temptation to retreat back into the arms of my addiction was overwhelming, but it was then that I swore that I would repay her with my sobriety. Wherever she had ascended to, I knew that that's what she would want most from me. At that point in my life, with everything else crashing down around me, I made a promise to myself—and to her—that I would never touch another opiate again.

A few months later, my life was finally starting to turn back around. Slowly and steadily, I had begun to climb my way out of the lake-sized grave I had been digging for myself the past few years. Then, one day on my lunch break as I was walking around downtown, I ran into an old friend who had also been a long-time heroin and opiate addict. After taking a good look at me and inquiring about my sobriety, he told me that he was now working for a local state-funded organization that works directly with people who are suffering from addiction to help them get connected with resources in their area. As luck would have it, a position in the company had just opened up and, provided I was stable in my recovery, the job would be mine. I was blown away by this seemingly chance encounter that offered what could be the opportunity of a lifetime. If there was even small chance that I could somehow turn my past addiction into something positive and make a difference in others' lives, then perhaps all those years of misery wouldn't be for nothing.

I sent in my resume and went for a brief interview. Another month passed, and I was told that I had the position. At this point I had under my belt the longest period of sobriety I'd ever achieved since I had started using. This accomplishment, along with the news that I now had this new job, only strengthened my resolve to stay clean. After all, I would now be working directly with people who were just like me; I had the opportunity to encourage, empower, and help them so that they too could put their addictions behind them. That special place in hell, or the terrible karmic forces that await those who continue to use while doing this type of job, did not interest me in the slightest.

Shortly after starting my new position, I realized that one of the most beneficial things a person can do while working on his or her own recovery is to surround him- or herself with others who are doing the same. One of the main reasons I was hired and given the chance to help others was that I knew first-hand what addiction was like. I had spent the better part of ten years living that life and, unlike so many, I had made it out to the other side. I could empathize with the people I was working to help, and sympathize with those who were in situations that were beyond my own personal experiences. Not only that, but everyone I was working with now had been hired for the same reason. We worked collectively as a unit with only one goal in mind: to help others in any way that we could, so that they could regain control of their addiction and get their lives back.

Some people reach out to us simply to talk. Others call in to get phone numbers for local detox and rehabilitation centers, or to get connected with a counselor or find a local Narcotics Anonymous meeting. Regardless, every individual who comes to us has only one thing in mind, and that's recovery. To this end, I am at her or his side through and through, for any step along the way.

For the first time in years, I feel a genuine sense of belonging. I absolutely love what I do and not only that, I am actually happy. With each day that passes, I become more stable in my sobriety. I continue to follow the plan that I set for myself in the weeks leading up to the death of my friend. I see a therapist and my Suboxone doctor monthly. I am sticking to my regimen and am talking with my doctor about my long-term plans and the gradual tapering off of the medication that has helped me stay sober. And while there are a lot of contributing factors to the success of my sobriety, I attribute much of it to the disciplined Suboxone regimen that I have stuck to. There's a lot of misinformation regarding the use of this drug, and many people look at the use of this medication as a simple substitute for the original substance that was being abused. While this may be the case for many, this is not the case for me. I am no longer getting high. My cravings and the temptations to relapse have almost entirely subsided. I am not going hungry or lying and stealing from my friends and family. Things are going great at my new job and I am now spending my free time doing the things I actually enjoy.

Every day, for eight hours a day, I spend the majority of my time speaking with and helping addicts and alcoholics, as well as their loved ones. Every call is different, and every single person is in a unique situation that they're desperately trying to find a way out of. Sadly, and not unlike myself, the vast majority of the people we help are suffering from addiction with opiates. Some found their way into addiction through a doctor's prescription. Others, like myself, were in the wrong place at the wrong time and simply made a mistake that they couldn't undo. The most heartbreaking of all are the mothers and fathers, the grandparents, or the significant others who call us looking to get their loved ones some help, but simply not knowing how to do so. The hardest truth of all for the majority of people that I speak with, is that the addiction that their loved one is going through is completely out of their hands.

To attain sobriety, to take control and get your life back from the throes of addiction, you have to truly want it. This is so easily said, but may arguably be one of the hardest things to actually do. If there's one thing that I've learned since starting this position and turning my life around, it's that everyone's path to recovery is different. What helps one user get clean may not work at all for another. Not only that, but there is no cure-all for addiction. There are dozens of little things that need to be done and changes that need to be made. Like breaking your leg and losing the ability to walk, recovery from addiction requires a tremendous amount of time, effort, and dedication to get back to the way things were before the break. And even then, most recovering addicts will have to live with and manage their addictions for the rest of their lives. That first hit, that one bag that I said *yes* to when I was seventeen, wreaked havoc on my life for almost ten years and left me with a lifetime of upkeep and more than my fair share of wrongs to try to right.

When I first made the choice to get clean, I was filled with regret for all the years of my life I had wasted, the harm that had been done to my body, the relationships that had been destroyed, and all the money I had recklessly spent chasing a high that I'd never again see. It wasn't until I was granted this opportunity to help others that I was able to reconcile myself with all of this. Every day I continue to help those who have found themselves where I once was. Each call is a firsthand reminder of why I continue to stay sober. Now, after a year in my position as a certified recovery specialist, I have nearly two full years sober under my belt—with absolutely no plans of going back.

❧

D. Ketchum works for a local nonprofit, helping individuals who are struggling with substance use issues get connected with resources in their area. He's currently working towards becoming a Certified Substance Abuse Counselor.

Good Morning, Death

— kerry rawlinson —

It's my vocation.

When a young mother demands cherry-red lipstick and garish eye-shadow for her sequined seven-year-old, adamant she'll exit earth as she'd entered beauty-pageants, I comply. When a gym-rat son, rippling with muscle and ink, challenges me to arm-wrestle for our most luxurious coffin at the lowest price, I don't. I once obliged an elderly harridan who insisted on keeping her late husband's dentures. She swore they'd cost too much to be burned. His ashes were returned, toothless.

You can't tell the core of hearts by their crusts, either. A brawny, walrus-mustached biker raced thirty-two hours to his brother's funeral, road-grimed, arms loaded with white roses, crying. His mother? Not a tear. Nobody can predict how grief will expose you.

Some may consider my vocation morbid, but I value its frankness. Death's schedule's unpredictable—and immediate. You can't postpone it. You can't write a sick-note, or take an All-Inclusive Cruise to avoid it. Hypocrisy's exposed. I'm a man of few words; I appreciate honesty. As my June says, the "silence runs deep" in me. I must discreetly execute the nitty-gritty business everybody sidesteps, soothe the broken-hearted, calmly repair ghoulish consequences of trauma. Needles and fillers; make-up. But I'm sympathetic to those desiring to exit the battle with as much dignity as can be mustered. Suffering is offensive. Which is why, every morning before preparing the newest client (my small eccentricity), I wryly acknowledge the whole business with "Good morning, Death."

The O'Reillys had an appointment today. They'd been fairly good friends years ago, before they monied, flying up to a tony address nestled in avenues of ancient trees, abandoning their roots. We lost touch. But Death reclaimed those roots, by handing me their son.

Daniel, back then, was a mischievous imp, routinely protesting innocence while pushing limits and buttons with equal vigor. Our own little Pippa came tripping indoors once, breathless.

"Daddy! Daniel says freckles are angels' kisses. Is that *true*? I could only chuckle.

"And, Daniel says because *I'm* an angel," she offered, "I have to kiss *every single freckle* of *his*!"

Though I seldom question Death's methods, I was upset at Daniel's end: Fentanyl.

Here's my dilemma. Over the last few months, my anecdotes fall on increasingly impassive ears. I'm home at precisely five-fifteen, as usual, relieving the day-nurse. I liquidize my June's supper, as usual; spoon it into her slack mouth. But her eyes no longer twinkle from my daily tales. No memory of freckles. Only a sudden, raucous ad from the TV's steady drone causes her to blink.

I ready her for sleep. I brush her hair, tying it with a lilac ribbon as she's done for decades, exposing her frail neck, lavender veins, her *foramen magnum*. After she settles, I snuggle

122

into her beloved nooks and crannies, now skeletal. I think about false teeth. I think about suffering—that of the living, alongside the dying. Angels' kisses. Death shall have a special "Good morning" soon. And the air-filled needle discreetly binned, with the all rest.

Hopeful

— Tom Pescatore —

Man, I'd love to sell all my percs.

if I wasn't crying by my bed on the floor for 6 hours every night
imagine what else I could be doing,
imagine what we could be using that money for—

Overpass

— Will Cordeiro —

Not the ash-blown starlight,
    not the loitering moon, not
        the lone wail

of a wolf, sounding out fields
    where someone's soon going
        to drape a tarp

over a body. Brother, no, it's just
    the dark itself—& that far-off
        glassy look you

gave, saying you were off to fetch
    a six-pack from the gas station
        that comes back

every time I pass the town's 24-hour
    WalMart where you boosted Oxy,
        its stocked shelves

like a mausoleum. The unseen suns
    within me flicker out, dim, souring
        in outsized signage

along the crumbling strip of midnight
  highway I cruise where every shadow
    has bred some demon.

Junky Obituary Newsfeed

— Nathanael Stolte —

Making an event page on Facebook the other night, I noticed that too many of my friends have passed away, many of them before they had seen thirty summers.

Maybe I should host a reading, invite only the dead, and see who shows up. Break out the homemade Ouija board, unpasteurized holy water, and salt distilled from the tears of the bereaved. We will all send up our poems together. Would Doug, Hollie, and James show up?

When I was in my first few months off the bug-juice, Doug was at the end of his second year. Doug was angry. He used to tell me he would never do heroin or touch a needle. It was beneath him. He was a secret crack-head; he thought he hid it well behind his knowledge of literature and his degree in English. It was his drinking, he said, that brought him to his knees. How quickly we lose our humility. Only took Doug twenty months. Watching him find fault, talk down to me and the other junk-boat-captains (captives), and eventually circle the drain, was a potent tonic. An example, an inspiration for a way I don't ever want to be. A few years later he came back, further damaged by John Barleycorn. There was just a little bit less of him—that's always the case—chemical attrition of the soul. He had fresh black and blue tracks on both arms and gaunt, sunken-in, slack face muscles—hallmarks of junk. I thought he had finally had enough. I thought he was done this time. I was wrong. Sometimes I hate being wrong. I wonder what he was thinking when he floated on his last nod. Sometimes we become what we loath. Sometimes we become what we fear.

Hollie lived in one of those houses on the West Side for sick broads. The drug-addled paper-dolls and the drunk out-and-down. I noticed right away that she wasn't looking for salvation. She was on the replacement plan; swapping the rig for an idol of tin and ash. Hollie didn't know what she was up against, hunted by The Jackal through the minefields of the heart. The fatal malady deludes the senses—how we deceive ourselves. She was sleeping around a lot. It sucks to say that about her—like I'm perverting her memory—but I won't tell lies about the dead. I wonder where her thoughts were when the ember faded, when she turned a junk shade of blue, when she left the broken-hearted behind. Often it is our joy that brings down the dirigible.

James was my friend, not just a kid I saw around. We broke bread together; we were ilk, spun from the same wheel. James was wicked smart, too smart. He couldn't grasp simple truths. I watched him go mad and dismantle his foundations. I'll take simplicity and mediocrity over crippling brilliance any day. James would call from time to time to tell me his woes. I was always pained to hear them but grateful he bothered to share. His father lived in the mountains of Western New York, out in ski country. Jimmy's father was a black-out daily drinker, also my ilk. He didn't have power or water that winter. He had drunk them away. In a black-out, he went outside for a shit, fell backwards into the snow with his pants around his ankles, and passed out. He froze to death in his own filth—God, let me die humble but not without dignity. Jimmy's papa died and he got some land. He called to ask me to pray for his mother; even though they were divorced, she was still hurt. He said to me, *God listens to you.* The next spring, Jimmy called to tell me he sold a chunk of land and was getting his check the following day. Sixty thousand dollars is a lot of coin for a junky. The last thing I said to him before we said goodbye was that if he didn't come back and let us help him he was going to die. There was no anger, only sorrow. The last time I saw him he was floating in a pine box of his mother's tears.

Truth can be ugly. Sometimes I hate being right.

Pyramids

— Damian Rucci —

The trailer park is
one hundred pyramids
of suburban decay

linoleum sided sarcophagi
bleached white by the
Bayshore sun

ambulances are chariots
without the lights on

no rush for the dead
who lay forgotten on
plastic covered furniture
while the news berates
their corpses with daily terrors

we worship the scarabs

the sons and daughters
of the trailer park pharaohs
who dance in the sun
and are revived with Narcan

I need to escape

Brother-in-law

— Jemshed Khan —

A redheaded boy rings doorbells
with a business card in one hand,
red wagon and key machine in tow.

He's fuels the gas mower by twelve:
Stripes lawns all summer long.
A neighbor sets out cold lemonade.

That first time he gulps red wine:
The Goldberg's Bar Mitzvah. Afterwards
he cuts a key to the liquor cabinet.

At sixteen, the Grateful Dead concert
adds whippets and weed to the mix up
with the downtown cops. Lawyers

get him off. By twenty he pushes
siding door to door: After hours, he downs
hard stuff and powders up in dirty bars.

He plasters hard-sell ads onto billboards:
1-800 numbers fronting St Louis Interstates.
Call now. Vinyl Siding. Operators standing by.

He pulls in real green, though
no luck with women. Forty finds him out
of the closet and into rehab.

His boy toys: breathalyzer on the ignition,
ankle bracelet, interlock. He lawyers up like OJ
as TV news gussies up a hit piece

on shifty business sharks. His folks find him:
basement blue, iced out on heroin cut with fentanyl.
The cops ask questions but no one knows.

Family clusters around fresh-dug ground
and lowers his casket into the rooted cellar,
buries him beneath the diamond cut lawn.

A Pharmacist's Choices and Their Impact on the Opioid Epidemic

— Alma McKinley, RPh —

The opioid epidemic has grown to such proportions that it no longer needs an introduction. Inundating people with numbers, graphs, scary lines, and horrific death tolls has already been done. All this information has served its purpose in waking us up to the sheer size of what it is we are facing together as a country, but it's still important to remember that behind every number and every bar graph there are people, human beings with stories. What I've come to realize in recalling my stories is that understanding the epidemic *intellectually* is so much easier than facing the role I played within it. I'm not a prescriber, nor do I work in any capacity for a pharmaceutical manufacturer. I'm not a drug dealer—not by traditional standards that is.

I am a pharmacist.

I became licensed in 1997, one year after a controlled-release form of oxycodone, touted as being non-addictive and the newest available treatment for a variety of chronic pains, was released on the market. I had no idea at the time that a compound, commonly known for its addiction potential, was being so egregiously misbranded. Retail pharmacy is such exhausting work that standing there all day juggling the demands of customers and doctors' offices made even the thought of going home and reading pharmacy journals and magazines too much to bear. Had I done it, I might have found one or more of Purdue's skillfully crafted ads. Ads that contained statements highlighting the positives of opioids in treating pain, like the fact that opioids had a long and trusted history of use in patients with cancer or terminal illnesses, were in large print and easy to read. Hiding in smaller font were the more questionable statements that claimed opioids were safe and effective for long-term use in treating non-cancerous pain. The latter claim was never proven in clinical trials at the time, but with the current epidemic we can draw our own conclusions in that matter. I'll always wonder, *what if?* Would have knowing any of this back then changed how I practiced? I'll never know the real answer, but I regretfully assume that, with the pressure from corporate to increase sales, along with being too tired and busy, that it wouldn't have.

What I know for sure is that I, quietly, played a part in one of the largest contributing factors to the epidemic we're facing today: the dispensing of heroin's legal counterpart, oxycodone, in all its forms. This is what it was like behind the numbers and statistics.

A Memory

It was early in the morning and her father was driving her down Pleasantville Road. Her parents were divorced and she had been living in the Bronx with her mom, when her father offered to move her to Briarcliff Manor because she had been hanging out with the wrong crowd, cutting classes, and getting dismal grades. She accepted, not knowing that moving to the 'burbs and changing high schools so she could attend Briarcliff High would be her own personal hell, while at the same time being her father's own personal triumph.

Her father had dubbed himself and his daughter as *The Paupers of Briarcliff.* They were surrounded by million-dollar houses, where everyone of legal driving age had a car. She and her father lived in a small, two-bedroom apartment and shared a vehicle, so the title fit. To say she was an outsider at school, her new social setting, was an understatement. She felt the sideways glances, heard all the whispers in the hallways, and finally caught on to the jocks taunting her with name calling muffled under coughs and the clearing of their throats. No one knew this was her daily truth but her.

Her father was driving with his right hand resting on the steering wheel at twelve o'clock, almost a defensive position as he had to look over his right shoulder to talk to her. His left arm was leaning on the door, and he was rubbing his chin with his left hand, decidedly calculating his next move. She knew all his tells and could sense something was brewing. Then he came out with it: "So, you know what you wanna major in when you go to college?"

"No." She was gazing out the window. She hadn't given this topic much thought, if any at all and, as a teenager "No" was a complete sentence.

Her father, on the other hand, had a lot invested in her. She was his last child of four, and the one he secretly hoped would fulfill his dreams of becoming a high-earning professional. His next statement was a reflection of all that desire overflowing, yet he played the scene out as coolly as he could, desperately trying to refrain from revealing the slightest attachment to what she did with her life. "I hear pharmacy is a nice, clean profession."

She continued to stare out the window, following the sun as it shimmered through the trees and blinded her off and on as the car made its way toward her school. The idea began to marinate right there in that moment and wasted no time taking shape.

Later that day, she went into her guidance counselor's office, but he wasn't there. She often wandered down to his office to escape or make it seem like she had something to do during free periods and oftentimes it was empty. Today she didn't mind because she was mostly there for The Book. The Book was like the phone directory of professions. You could look up any major or job alphabetically and find out how many years of school it required and any other prerequisites it needed, along with how much the average yearly salary was. It was an outdated book, as school reference books tend to be, but the numbers after the dollar sign next to the word *pharmacist* looked good to her. She thought to herself, *That'll do just fine.*

A little over a decade later, I was a pharmacist standing at the drive-through window of a Walgreen's pharmacy. I had Alice's profile pulled up on the computer in front of me and her prescription resting on the easel. Each time I saw her I would tell myself, *I'm not going to fill for her anymore,* but then I would go right on ahead and fill it again anyway. I don't know what made this day any different from the others. I suppose my frustration with doctor-shoppers and pill-seekers had reached its limit. I was only five years into what would be an eighteen-year-long career. I think I refused Alice more out of curiosity to see how it would feel, how would it play out and, of course, I was certain I was justified given the evidence in her profile. "I can't fill this for you"—that was all I said that first time I refused to fill an opioid prescription.

"What? Why?"

This interaction was awkward to begin with because Alice sat in car on the other side of a pane of glass and I was talking to her on a microphone. The idea that every barrier you put between you and the patient takes away from effective communication was something I learned in my Interpersonal Communications class and, in moments like these, that message rang loud and true inside my mind.

Alice was in her seventies. She was tiny and frail, but she drove a boat of a car. How she got around barely seeing over the steering wheel I'll never know. Her car was the scariest thing about her. She always wore a bad wig, which made me wonder if she had cancer. I think I was able to confront her, unlike the other addicts who came by, for one simple reason: she was smaller than I. I could take her if I had to, but I also knew it would never come to that. Alice would never come inside the store—she was strictly drive-through. I guess deep down I knew if I was going to make an example of someone, put my foot down with any of these users, she was my safest bet.

"Alice, I can't fill this because you've never seen the same doctor twice. Each time you come through here you've got another prescription for Percocet and it's always written by a new doctor. If I'm going to continue to fill these for you, then I have to know you are under the treatment of one physician who is following your care. I'm sorry."

I said I was sorry, but I really wasn't. I was pissed. I was tired of being taken advantage of, tired of people thinking that I had to fill their scripts just because a doctor wrote them. The notion that I just sat in this box of a pharmacy all day long at their beck and call, bound to fill any nonsense a doctor wrote on a piece of paper, was annoying most days and infuriating on the worst ones.

"But my back pain," she said with a pleading tone.

"One doctor Alice. Does each of these doctors know about the others?"

Alice had filled dozens of prescriptions for generic Percocet 10/325 from our pharmacy for various quantities. That's 10 mg of oxycodone and 325 mg of acetaminophen (APAP), the active ingredient in Tylenol. If Alice didn't die from her oxycodone addiction, her liver would give out from the Tylenol. I wasn't going to feed the junkie habit of an elderly women who was washed up because of back pain. No: with Alice I drew the line, a line I would let so many others cross for years to come.

Alice looked out over her steering wheel, staring out into space. She blinked. Was she considering that? Was she calculating her next steps? I wasn't sure. What I did know for certain was that I had just disrupted her pattern. She always came through the drive-through after five o'clock, dropped off her prescription, and came back to pick it up in thirty minutes.

Though I had reached my limit, saying "No" wasn't easy to do. My body seemed to be running away from my rational mind. My heart was racing—it felt like a rabbit's hind legs trying to beat a hole straight through the center of my chest. Adrenalin rushed through my veins and my hands trembled. And this was just Alice.

In the silence between us that seemed to stretch never-ending, I took a breath, hoping this was going to go the way I wanted it to, that she would drive away and not come back. She did.

∂

A few years later, I was tucked away in the pharmacy, sitting hunched over on a low step stool, reading a book that rested on my knees. I was hidden from view by the aisles of drugs that surrounded me. There I sat, alone and drinking a Diet Coke, working the third shift for Walgreens in Aurora, Colorado. I had taken the job to have flexibility to travel to Florida often because my father was diagnosed with cancer. He had since passed, and then I kept the job because of all of this solitude. It was so much better than the frenzy in the pharmacy that existed during the day.

Then I heard the rustling sound at the counter that indicated someone was there and I would have to get up. I sighed. The mere act of standing up out of this hunched but comfortable position was a burden. It was even more so when I only had to do it about every hour or two at best.

As I turned the corner I thought, *Good God, what now?*

I approached the man standing there. He was young, white, and had blood rushing down his face. His shirt was already soaked. I took the paper from this man's extended arm and put it on the easel in front of me. *Nice, clean profession.* The fresh blood, from a clearly recent injury, was literally gushing from his nose. The script had his fingerprint in blood on one corner. He held his hand up to his face, making a half-hearted attempt to conceal what was already an out-of-control, bloody mess.

Some people I just didn't have to talk to. In the middle of the night, a "Hi, how can I help you?" seemed like a vacuous way to greet him. He knew why he was here and so did I.

But as I stood there taking in this prescription it was as if every part of my being was trying to send me a message. My brain went from leisurely passing the time to high alert in an instant, and now came to a screeching halt. My stomach was in knots and my fingers, usually gliding effortlessly across the keyboard to pull up the patient and begin entering the prescription were stuck, refusing to type. I knew better than to try and ignore this feeling in my gut. A bad vibe during the hustle and bustle of the day would signal that I should double-check the script in my hand, and I would always find a mistake in it that would have been easy to miss. This bad feeling at this time of night could only mean one thing: he had given me a fake prescription.

He noticed my hesitation. He said, "Um, I'm sorry about the mess. Is there a problem?"

It was a Percocet prescription, written on an Exempla Emergency Department blank. I realized three things all

140

at once: sixty tablets from an emergency room was a really high quantity; this wasn't the first fake prescription in recent weeks from this particular ER; and this guy had just broken his own nose in the parking lot to rush me into filling it. I was pissed. I tried calling the ER when he was out of sight, but I had to leave a message. The whole scene was so surreal, I wanted nothing more than to extract myself from it and be done with him. I overrode my gut, my instincts, and filled it. In situations like this that were all too familiar, I had to choose between sidestepping the facts and my instincts and filling scripts out of external pressure to do so, or gearing up for the conflict I envisioned occurring when, or if, I would refuse to fill the prescription. Neither choice felt particularly good and both left me exhausted and disenchanted with the path I had chosen. This was no way to make a living.

Andrew was another night-time regular. He had a problem. I knew that despite all I ever said to him was *Hi*, *Okay*, and *Here you go*. Every script I ever filled for him was for oxycodone-acetaminophen 5 mg/325 mg. Each script was written legitimately by an emergency room physician, a different doctor almost every time. On the occasions that I would call to inform these doctors that this kid had a problem, I was told their script was fine. It was interactions like this that made me doubt myself:

"Well, he has an abscessed tooth. I'm not sure how you would fake something like that," the doctor would add. I didn't know either, but I knew that there was no way Andrew could fake one for the many months he was getting Percocet prescriptions. What other conditions was he making up? I knew he had a problem, and I was trying to do something, the only thing I knew how to do: get the doctor to cancel the prescription. The doctors didn't want to leave Andrew without pills to treat his pain; they saw no issue with their prescription for only ten or fifteen tablets, so they let their orders stand. And Andrew got his habit fed.

Andrew was a Goth. He always wore black jeans with a dark hoodie covering his greasy hair, his lips blood red against his pallid skin. I never knew what color his eyes really were because he wore Marilyn Manson white-out contact lenses over them. The lenses always freaked me out. He was good at keeping to just the transaction. His garb protected him well, his eyes making it impossible to hold his glance. He always smiled at the end, like he thought it was the polite thing to do.

But he was someone's son. He had a mother. I wondered if she knew where her son was at night. Did she care? I like to think there were people who cared about him. That would let me off the hook.

When I remember Andrew, I regret never speaking to him about his habit. I never took a moment to go beyond our transaction and inquire about his life, his relationships, and the years ahead of him that, hopefully, he would be around to see. Andrew made his choices and I made mine by remaining silent. The nature of this job had long since beaten away any desire to counsel anyone. Sure, when I was asked I would offer my professional advice, but when it came to opiates, I kept my opinions to myself. As a graveyard pharmacist, a woman alone in the back of a store, I filled the scripts just so that the customers would leave. Working for years filling two hundred to two hundred fifty prescriptions during the day, I was just trying to keep my head above water. I kept my nose to the grind stone, rarely looking up at the collateral damage standing in the waiting room waiting for their drugs. After seven years I was completely desensitized to what I was doing. I stopped watching the news around 2003, and the only reason I knew there was a problem with opiates was because I saw it every day in my job.

These scenes aren't the worst; they don't even begin to scratch the surface of what it's like at the pharmacy counter everyday across America. After stepping away from the counter for good, three years ago, I found myself finally getting the education I wish I had had back then on the epidemic. I was reading articles, books, and government reports, attending conferences, and revisiting my own experiences, like the ones I've shared here, and my mind began to change. As a pharmacist, I had the world of pain meds divided into *us* and *them,* the pharmacy staff versus the ones addicted to the drugs. My choices were limited to filling the prescription or not. In hindsight, what I see is a systemic failure to see the person, to connect in a more human way, instead of focusing solely on the transaction.

Unfortunately, that transactional process is very much the current expectation in the drug store. There is so much more opportunity un-mined in those moments at the pharmacy. For instance, if pharmacists were educated on what addiction really is, a substance use disorder and a treatable disease, that shift alone could potentially lead to different outcomes. It might help remove stigmas around the disorder and barriers to communication and the chance, however small, of meaningful connection. Similar to undiagnosed diabetics, there are hundreds of thousands, if not millions, suffering on some level with substance use disorder and they are unaware that it is operating within them and that there are options that can help them. In fact, training pharmacists on how to authentically engage with these patients to get a conversation started would be a grand opportunity for not only opening up more access points to treatment, but in building trust between these two groups of people. These two changes alone would have opened up my choices from beyond the only two I felt I had and given me a chance to effect some improvement in the lives of the people I encountered.

❧

Alma McKinley graduated from Massachusetts College of Pharmacy in June 1997. Thus began her career as a retail pharmacist that took her from the suburbs of Boston, to West Palm Beach, Florida, and her permanent residence outside Denver, Colorado. She is married and has two children, a pre-teen and a kindie. When Alma was five years old and she knew how to write her alphabet, she was enamored with writing letters, marrying them in any order, for the mere act of writing brought her joy. Today, writing continues to be her passion and is as essential to her life as the air she breathes. She draws her inspiration from nature, long walks, birds, her children's faces, anything that allows her to lose herself in the moment and draw from divine inspiration. Her first, finished essay was the result of a creative non-fiction writing class this past fall, where she wrote about her career as a pharmacist.